Miss Marple:
Christian Sleuth

Miss Marple:
Christian Sleuth

Isabel Anders

Winchester, UK
Washington, USA

First published by Circle Books, 2013
Circle Books is an imprint of John Hunt Publishing Ltd., Laurel House, Station Approach,
Alresford, Hants, SO24 9JH, UK
office1@jhpbooks.net
www.johnhuntpublishing.com
www.circle-books.com

For distributor details and how to order please visit the 'Ordering' section on our website.

Text copyright: Isabel Anders 2012

ISBN: 978 1 78099 543 4

A CIP catalogue record for this book is available from the British Library.

Design: Stuart Davies

Printed and bound by CPI Group (UK) Ltd, Croydon, CR0 4YY

We operate a distinctive and ethical publishing philosophy in all
areas of our business, from our global network of authors to
production and worldwide distribution.

CONTENTS

The detective is a prophet looking backwards.
– Ellery Queen

To Diane Marquart Moore
Poet and sleuth extraordinaire

Miss Marple: A Force to Reckon With

Time and trouble will tame an advanced young woman, but an advanced old woman is uncontrollable by any earthly force.
– Dorothy L. Sayers

The righteous flourish like the palm tree... In old age they still produce fruit.
– Psalm 92:12a, 14a

As my husband and I have been watching dramatizations of various detective series through the years, we've found that they offer more than brainy entertainment. Escape, certainly, from one's own issues and struggles. Answers to mysteries that make one feel that the problems of the world can be understood and intelligently dealt with. Satisfying resolutions within a limited scope and time frame.

But we've also experienced a nagging or pulling toward *deeper* meaning through these watchings, an issue which we often discuss. In fact, it seems that without straining or deliberate effort to 'find meaning', my mind simply goes on probing the knottier issues around *what it means to deal in discernment of good and evil* – and to enable the good to win out.

And always, as we skip around among the various episodes available on DVD – usually watching one per evening – it is the plain, intelligent, earnest face of the elderly actress Joan Hickson as Miss Marple (author Agatha Christie's own favorite choice for the role) that moves me the most.

What is it about the "old lady with a sweet, placid, spinsterish face" that strikes such a chord of spiritual recognition? Perhaps it is simply the realization that the least likely person in the room holds the key to the most entangled mystery – the one that others have failed to solve.

But is she really so tame and innocuous? Similar to C.S. Lewis' character of Aslan in his Narnia series, who, it is pointed out, is not a "tame" lion – Miss Marple herself might be genteel, soft-spoken, self-contained, and a proper English gentlewoman. But as Christie's stories about her so cunningly reveal, she is far from 'safe'. As her housekeeper Cherry comments in *Nemesis:* "Anyone would think you were gentle as a lamb. But there's times I could say you'd behave like a lion…" if the circumstances called for it.

In the words of the St. Mary Mead vicar, Leonard Clement, the narrator of Miss Marple's literary debut, 1930s *Murder at the Vicarage:* "Miss Marple is a white-haired old lady with a gentle, appealing manner – Miss Wetherby [her neighbor] is a mixture of vinegar and gush. Of the two Miss Marple is the more dangerous."

But dangerous to whom – and in what ways leonine – or heroic? If the theme of a successful murder mystery is 'truth will out', then Miss Marple clearly reveals herself to be perpetually on the side of that winning quality. Yet she achieves her successes not by innocent credulity, but rather (similar to Father Brown in the Chesterton stories) by discerning good and evil and under-standing how they are often manifested in individuals and the world. She knows what signs to be wary of in human behavior, and her acute observations, practiced in her home village of St. Mary Mead and beyond, bear that out.

She admits at various times through the books: "It is dangerous to believe people. I haven't for years…" According to Anne Hart in *The Life and Times of Miss Jane Marple*, "She also believed very strongly in justice of the old-fashioned kind… To her, evil was evil."

She might even shake one of her ubiquitous knitting needles to emphasize a point. But she is also able to keep a secret, to wait until the opportune time to reveal what she *does* know – or even intentionally to mislead. "Miss Marple had been brought up to have a proper regard for truth and was indeed by nature a very truthful person. But on certain occasions, when she considered it her duty to do so, she could tell lies with a really astonishing verisimilitude," Hart points out.

Balancing all of these character traits found in the novels leads, I believe, to a fascinating, full-bodied portrait of Jane Marple not only as a Christian sleuth – but as *a woman for others in her own particular time and place.*

I hope to show, through examples in the Christie books centered on this heroine detective, some ways in which even our most mundane actions toward each other can have immense, long-lasting consequences for good or evil. And I also will explore the implications of her example for our own Christian lives among others.

Another lesson inherent in the ordinariness of Miss Marple could be that *we are all making impressions* in one way or the other when we are least aware of it. The character of Miss Marple has had this effect on me, provoking much questioning and pondering. As Thomas Merton said, "One of the first signs of a saint will be the fact that other people do not know what to make of him" – or her. What will we make of her life?

This quiet, unobtrusive old lady who always read a few devotional lines of Thomas à Kempis' *Imitation of Christ* in bed before turning out the light, who asserted in old age that "I believe in eternal life," surely qualifies as a quiet saint among her peers. And through reading the stories, those who 'get her' will find small windows of truth that can lead to greater insights as to *how to live* ourselves.

In an example of classic understatement in the short story "The Thumbmark of St. Peter", in which Miss Marple also says, "I connected the two things together, faith – and fish," she modestly admits: "It is true, of course, that I have lived what is called a very uneventful life, but I have had a lot of experiences in solving different little problems that have arisen."

Arguably, a meaningful life IS one in which just such small victories of order and truth over chaos add up to the saving of others – allowing them to go on with their lives in peace and safety, or to be revealed in their true character. These are typical results of Miss Marple's actions, once her solution of a crime puts everything in perspective.

To me, what follows in this study is not simply a compendium of a fictional character's acts for our admonition. Seeing Miss Marple as Christian sleuth is an exercise in studying the novels about her with new intent: to illuminate a dimension of her character that has not previously been featured on its own.

However, the body of work which forms the text of our study is not, after all, a complete or internally consistent secondary world. Certainly there are within this fictional landscape an inordinate number of subterfuges, false representations, malice and actual murders than would be probable within St. Mary Mead's small population, even over the several decades of Miss Marple's career. And, aside from the 'unpleasantness' of these incidents, the little English village, both in the books and movie adaptations, can seem impossibly quaint and nearly removed from time, its comfortable assumptions and reliable customs only tentatively challenged. Often it seems to be merely a cozy backdrop to the world's larger troubles.

But I believe that, within it, important lessons lie.

What I want to uncover and expand on in these chapters are some ways in which the character of Miss Marple in the texts suggests *a pattern for grace-filled, redemptive practices* that we also can follow.

She is a woman for others...

She manages to do good from exactly the point where she is 'planted'...

She recognizes the God-given value in other people and sees them as her neighbors for whom she bears responsibility...

She is a firm believer in truth in both its transcendent and immanent forms...

She is sincerely humble and does not act in order to draw attention to herself or to gain worldly reward – besides the fact that staying 'under the radar' as a nearly invisible person enables her craft...

She is uncannily perceptive at sizing up a situation, discerning clues, working from analogies and past experiences to deduce probabilities. She is adept at untangling knotty cases through her sharp-as-a-razor intellect...

She, though a spinster, believes heartily in love, honors those who express it healthily on all levels, and sees it as redemptive...

In short, she demonstrates enough Christlike understanding and actions to lead us to conclude that Miss Marple is truly a 'woman for others', worthy of another look. In fact, she could be seen as a sort of living parable herself, through her many mystery cases, observations, and personal modeling of healing love.

Why do modern readers continually return to the St. Mary Mead of nearly a century ago to enjoy the stories about this modest, unassuming woman – in a world of super-action heroes, novels that explore and exploit supernatural powers, over-the-top lifestyles, and in-your-face defiance of order and justice?

Perhaps as a relief, a correction, a respite? Contrast always helps to paint extremes in clearer light.

I only know that her inclusion in the pantheon of iconic sleuths seems secure. I believe that Miss Marple's unique mind and spirit offer a valuable perspective that could easily be lost in the rush and flash of more overt manipulations in the world. Does it have something to do with her being a woman of a certain age?

As *New York Times* columnist Gail Collins recently wrote:

We're a long way from the Eleanor Roosevelt Commission on

the Status of Women, which was formed when there were no women on the White House staff doing anything more impressive than typing or cake decoration. "Men have to be reminded that women exist," Mrs. Roosevelt tartly told reporters.

Miss Marple not only reminds us that women are important to the fabric of civilized society, but also that old age is not to be scorned or underestimated when it comes to wisdom and truth being perpetuated in important ways.

Let her creep into your consciousness, as she has mine, through her sleuthing actions that come 'on little cat feet', amid cups of tea and perpetual knitting. Once evil gets its due, restorative – sometimes nearly *redemptive* – results will not be far behind.

A Woman for Others

For Dietrich Bonhoeffer, Jesus is the "man for others."...He exists for us today in and through the community of saints.
– Richard P. McBrien

The Thomas à Kempis fan club includes St. Ignatius, Thomas Merton, Thomas More, and even Agatha Christie's Miss Marple. (She reads a chapter of The Imitation of Christ *every night before sleep.)*
– Michael Joseph Gross

Do not show partiality, to your own harm, or deference, to your downfall. Do not refrain from speaking at the proper moment, and do not hide your wisdom.
– Sirach 4:22–23

One central question driving this study of Agatha Christie's creation, Miss Marple – her character, her acts, and her meaning – is, for me: *what does she get* out of her many selfless contributions to the welfare of the lives of others within her fictional world?

What is the payoff? *How* can she give and give, and so seemingly effortlessly enter in to the fray, not counting the personal cost of becoming involved in dangerous situations? From whence comes her devotion to the Good and her single-minded dedication to the success of others' lives? What spiritual resources sustain her, and bring her to the level of representing 'a woman for others' —in Jesus' example?

In the twelve Miss Marple novels and the twenty stories, Jane Marple's intelligence and perseverance are crucial not only for individuals who are suffering from the effects of a threat or a crime — but for the *whole society*, both localized and extended. For her fictional world, like the real one, requires an equilibrium, a resolution, a balance in order to endure. This truth is often expressed in the stories in the most down-to-earth, concrete details.

At the end of *The Body in the Library*, the 'dance' of life goes on, symbolized by a minor character's return to the ballroom for another 'round'. In the wrap-up of *The Moving Finger*, the nature of a relationship is confirmed with humor and irony as a character's 'little joke' takes on the form of an unconventional wedding present.

It is understood by any reader who inhabits the pages of these mystery novels for very long that St. Mary Mead desperately requires its essential tranquility – for however long it can last until the next upset occurs. Without this tension, a pattern of disruption and eventual resolution, the stories would not work as well as they do.

Within this setting, the central character Jane Marple is clearly depicted as a loyal and dedicated Anglican churchwoman. Thus she can be expected to be consistently on the side of the Good. In some of her reminiscences she mentions two of her uncles, the 'canons', one who was Canon of Chichester Cathedral and the other of Ely Cathedral.

There is a strong church ethic underlying not only the village itself, but Miss Marple's implied history, though the older members of her family are presumably long dead. Although there are repeated comments about Miss Marple not having gotten out of St. Mary Mead very often in her life, there is in *They Do It with Mirrors* a mention of her having grown up in a cathedral close. Was she herself, like Dorothy Sayers (a contemporary of Agatha Christie and fellow mystery writer), the daughter of a clergyman?

We are also told that she was sent at about the age of sixteen to a finishing school in Florence, Italy, where she met two American girls, Ruth and Carrie Louise Martin. When the three of them again met up in their later years, Ruth reminded them of their early ideals: "You were going to nurse lepers, Jane, and I was going to be a nun. One gets over all that nonsense." But as the novels reveal, Jane was destined to channel her innate altruism in other, equally dangerous ways to nursing lepers.

Certainly through her life she was, and continued to be, a regular churchgoer. She also is shown to have accepted her share of parish responsibilities. This rubber-meets-the-road servanthood was an appropriate way of expressing her love of God and neighbor, one far more fitting for a Victorian-styled lady than much open discussion of God or theology would have been.

Taking hints from a list in *The Body in the Library*, some of her parish-related activities might have included: raising funds for the Nave Restoration Fund, St. Giles' Mission, the Sale of Work, the Fund for Unmarried Mothers, the Boy Scouts, the Needlework Guild, and the Bishop's Appeal for Deep Sea Fishermen! [She assumes one or more of these collection duties, with the help of the vicar's wife, as a 'cover' in order to circulate unsuspected among parishioners while investigating the case.]

She also supported the Women's Institute and the Orphanage Committee, and would have helped organize the 'jumble sales' that raised money for various charities. As Puritan sympathizer Miss Ramsbottom in *A Pocket Full of Rye* grudgingly admits, "She's frivolous, like all Church of England people, but she knows how to run a charity in a sensible way."

According to Anne Hart, author of *The Life and Times of Miss Jane Marple*: "The most important creed in her life was simply to do one's duty. But she did say once, 'Now, I dare say you modern young people will laugh, but when I am in really bad trouble I always say a little prayer... And I always get an answer.'"

As Thomas à Kempis (ca. 1380–1471) wrote: "Never be

entirely idle; but either be reading, or writing, or praying or meditating or endeavoring something for the public good." This ideal, perhaps reread often in her little devotional book at nighttime prayers, certainly circumscribed her life.

Perhaps the most difficult point for younger readers of these works to grasp is how *undivided* her early twentieth-century world was, compared to ours today. Though the "young people" listening to her in the books might have thought Miss Marple a bit of an anachronism even then, British society in general was much more of one mind about what constituted moral (and immoral) behavior. Aberrations such as adultery, theft, graft, blackmail, assault, and even murder occurred fairly frequently as eruptions in the placid village life Christie depicted so well. But they were always understood to be ugly outcroppings of evil, malicious interruptions that impeded livable life. And in Christie's world they couldn't blithely be explained away by unfortunate parental upbringing or other unfair past treatment toward the perpetrators.

Miss Marple once revealed (in *Nemesis*) her own hard stand against evil with regard to a young murderer who had been caught: "If you expect me to feel sympathy, regret, urge an unhappy childhood [in defense], blame bad environment... I do not feel inclined so to do."

But Miss Marple did engage her intelligence and God-centered compassion in ways that could help prevent just such society-wrecking outcomes. In several stories she is depicted as employing young women from a nearby orphanage to come work for her. Even though it requires more of her time and training than would hiring an experienced maid, she patiently instructs these less fortunate souls in general housekeeping, enduring their mistakes as they try to learn a gentlewoman's standards for maintaining a tight household. Sometimes this ongoing charitable work of hers figures into her involvement in and solving of a crime.

More than this, there are several stories in which Miss Marple's own proactive and courageous actions actually rescue the lives of others. In *Sleeping Murder*, for instance, she saves a victim from strangling by squirting a stream of soapy water (fresh from garden use) into the would-be-killer's eyes. She is not afraid either to set traps (sometimes involving younger accomplices, as in *The Moving Finger*) or even of putting herself out as bait to help catch a perpetrator.

Though she is not herself aristocratic, she was greatly at home among the landed and the privileged, often staying through various circumstances at grand homes surrounded by ancestral acreage and estate properties. She has never worked herself, but exists on some kind of fixed income (probably from family inheritance), enhanced by assistance from her famous nephew Raymond West (presumably her late sister's son), a successful novelist who appears in a number of the Marple novels and stories.

She is able to receive this help graciously, and also to give generously to others when the occasion requires it. In the novel *4.50 from Paddington* (also known as *What Mrs. McGillicuddy Saw*), Jane Marple spends her own money to help her friend Elspeth McGillicuddy take train trips with her to pin down the place where a murdered body would have been dumped off the train; enlists the expensive (but worth it) assistance of a young domestic manager, Lucy Eyelesbarrow, supplementing the young woman's salary to include her contributions as a sleuth, as Lucy works undercover in a suspect household.

And not only her money, but also Miss Marple's time and energy were available to be put to use when Christian duty required it. As is noted in *A Caribbean Mystery*: "Like many old people she slept lightly and had periods of wakefulness which she used for the planning of some action or actions to be carried out on the next or following days." Hers, by choice, was far from a 'quiet life'. The stakes of human rescue were too high.

Her generosity with time and willingness to engage in difficult cases meant that she was not only underestimated because of her plain looks and gentlewomanly manner: "Modesty forbade Miss Marple to reply that she was, by now, quite at home with murder," we read in *They Do It with Mirrors*. She was also required in various cases to carry that modesty even further by deferring to professional investigators when they found her presence tiresome – and, though perhaps unconsciously, a threat to their own self-importance and perceived skills.

Moments of truth about Miss Marple's worth as a sleuth inevitably arise during the process of criminal investigations, in spite of these rivalries and fears. Colonel Melchett, chief constable of St. Mary Mead's surrounding county, was "an irascible-looking man with a habit of tugging at his short red moustache." He oversaw a number of murders that Miss Marple was able to solve in her sideline way, not always taking the law into her confidence. But the gruff Colonel was forced to admit: "She's a very sharp old lady."

She often responded to such a compliment in her typical self-effacing way: "Really I'm not at all clever – just, perhaps, a *slight* knowledge of human nature – living, you know, in a *village*."

Indeed. For these stories usually begin and end with scenes from normal village life, providing a circular flow through chaos to equilibrium that is always dependent on how the principal residents act to, and for, and against each other. And as one of her housekeepers responds when Miss Marple thanks her, saying, "You take very good care of me, Cherry": "Got to. Good people are scarce."

Miss Marple's plain speaking and straightforward acting is also described by another public crime-fighting official as making her "The most frightening woman I ever met." What is her secret? How does she manage to zero in on exactly what needs to done for another's welfare?

A translation of the Wisdom book of Sirach (4:22–23) by Rabbi Rami Shapiro goes: "Be detached from your own welfare, and impartial when considering others. Do not stay silent when speech is called for, nor abandon the world to hide in spirit." A beautifully accurate description of Miss Marple's *modus operandi*.

But Jane Marple remains a paradox. Which is she? Simply good or frankly frightening? Are spiritually honed goodness and an other-directed life necessarily a threat to the status quo? If so, then Miss Marple is an unlikely embodiment BOTH of the *gadfly*, annoying others into doing the right thing or accepting the consequences – *and* of the overseeing mother figure who wants to see all of the 'children' playing fairly.

As the Rev. Leonard Clement says in *The Murder at the Vicarage*:

> Of all the ladies in my congregation, I consider her by far the shrewdest. Not only does she see and hear practically every-thing that goes on, but she draws amazingly neat and apposite deductions from the facts that come under her notice. If I were at any time to set out on a career of deceit, it would be of Miss Marple that I should be afraid.

With great discipline and intelligence, she seems able to keep the details of any given case before her as she goes about her expected quotidian tasks. Yet she is ready to apply her findings like the turn of a screw to nail villains in the end.

And, it could be argued, she also operates on a spiritual level: seeing the world, represented by St. Mary Mead (in most stories) as a battleground between the forces of good and evil.

When another character in the story *The Sittaford Mystery* suggests that a house itself might contain evil, Miss Marple replies: "The house is bricks and mortar. If there's evil, it's in somebody's heart."

Yet, when a murderer is identified, she does not step up to

claim any kind of personal credit. At the end of *The Murder at the Vicarage*, "Naturally nothing was said [at the trial] of Miss Marple's share in the business. She herself would have been horrified at the thought of such a thing." This humble reticence almost qualifies as "not letting the left hand know what the right hand is doing," as per Jesus' injunction in the Gospels.

How can we measure this genuine modesty and these gentle gifts in any other way than to see Miss Marple as essentially a Christian figure from the core? She humbly accepts her societal status and embraces the reality of her meager financial resources, giving thanks in many instances for them, and sharing them as she is able – overall reminiscent of a boy's gift of five loaves of bread and two fish that Jesus expanded into a legendary feast.

Surely this is the way of selflessness, the way 'a woman for others' in any time or place would naturally conduct her life and mind her soul – actions for which she answers only to God.

Miss Marple, like the feminine figure of Wisdom itself in the Old Testament Proverbs, walks "in the way of righteousness, along the paths of justice" (8:20). Her generous actions and self-forgetting deeds are healing ones and – in God's use of all our gifts – are expanded like leavened loaves to serve not only the immediate beneficiaries of justice, but the good of the larger world.

Thus is Miss Marple an exemplary figure for others, following in Christ's own pattern.

Thomas à Kempis quotes (read "woman" along with "man"):

The more a man is united within himself and interiorly simple, the more and higher things doth he understand without labour; because he receiveth the light of understanding from above.

The good devout man first makes inner preparation for the actions he has later to perform. His outward actions do not draw him into lust and vice; rather it is he who bends them into the shape of reason and right judgment. Who has a stiffer battle to fight than the man who is striving to conquer himself?

First keep the peace within yourself, then you can also bring peace to others.

Questions for Discussion:

1 Which of Miss Marple's actions within her books speak to you most of her Christlike attributes?
2 What other qualities in her would you compare to those of Christ in his earthly life?
3 Which Gospel parables most readily come to your mind in relation to Miss Marple and her selflessness? What does the author's (Agatha Christie's) depiction of her particularity in her time and place add to your understanding of these Gospel truths?
4 What does it mean to you to "imitate" Christ in your daily walk?

2

Solitude, Focus, and Knitting

As The Imitation of Christ *explains, "unless you like solitude it is
not safe for you to appear in public"* (Bk. I, ch. 20)
– Opus Sanctorum Angelorum

*God is the friend of silence. See how nature – trees, flowers, grass –
grows in silence; see the stars, the moon and the sun, how they move
in silence... We need silence to be able to touch souls.*
– Mother Teresa

Openness, patience, receptivity, solitude is everything.
– Rainer Maria Rilke

How does Miss Marple's 'centeredness' in her life in St. Mary
Mead reflect Jesus' own singular life of solitude and ministry?
How can an old woman's sitting, knitting, thinking, praying –
even be compared to it? Jesus himself used quite far-flung illus-
trations to teach the truth of the Kingdom to his followers: a
fruitless fig tree, a merchant buying a field, the play of children,
the catching of fish.

As Joan Chittister has pointed out in *Becoming Fully Human*, it
is in the small things that greatness is mirrored, macrocosm to
microcosm:

Every spiritual master in every tradition talks about the signif-
icance of small things in a complex world. Small actions in
social life, small efforts in the spiritual life, small moments in
the personal life. All of them become great in the long run, the
mystics say, but all of them look like little or nothing in
themselves.

To quote from Jesus' parable of the talents, a faithful servant is told: "You have been trustworthy in a few things, I will put you in charge of many things; enter into the joy of your master" (Mt 25:23).

Vision begins here – from this Christian conception of discipleship that requires silence, centering, discipline. The fruit of its practice can produce tenfold, twentyfold, a hundredfold, as is borne out in the cases of Miss Marple going about her business of being herself in the world.

Her detective operations, of course, will involve *both* silent, inner focus – *and* outer garrulousness at appropriate times, engaging in what appears to be spinsterly gossip, for a purpose. Both methods are shown in the Marple books to yield results. As Edward Gibbon observed, "Conversation enriches the understanding, but solitude is the school of genius."

Miss Marple, from her various descriptions in the novels and stories, is well characterized as a person of solitude. She lives alone, with usually no more than one domestic helper in residence. She spends her time in quiet pursuits, reading, reflecting, drinking cups of tea (or occasionally sherry), accomplishing small tasks, and perpetually knitting something (usually pink and fluffy) for the younger generations. But she is never painted by Christie as one to be pitied. Rather, her aloneness and solitary stance clearly nurture a richness of soul, and even at times the flaming out of detective genius.

A passage in *A Caribbean Mystery* describes how Miss Marple "took out her knitting and her needles and clicked rapidly as though they were trying to match the speed of her thoughts. She didn't like it, no, she didn't like it..." This correlation of a sedentary occupation that uses one's hands, with the ruminative musings of a first-class brain (in the same person) is a brilliant matching of similar-but-different movements. Together they delineate a unique and admirable balance between body and soul in this elderly woman.

Readers soon discover that Jane Marple's habit of deductive reflection, like her busy hands, can be accomplishing much when it looks as though she is simply fulfilling a stereotypical role in polite society. Patricia Craig and Mary Cadogan in *The Lady Investigates: Women Detectives and Spies in Fiction* wrote in a chapter on "Grandmotherly Disguise": "Knitting, although it has sinister connotations which go back to Madame Defarge and the knitters round the guillotine, chiefly represents feminine industry and apparent harmlessness." And it can be done quietly, in private.

There is another dimension to solitude as well. Anthony Storr writes in his book *Solitude*:

> The Victorian lady used regularly to retire for a 'rest' in the afternoon. She needed to do so because convention demanded that she should constantly be empathically alert to the needs of others without regard to any needs of her own. Her afternoon rest allowed her to recuperate from the social role of dutiful listener and ministering angel; a role which allowed no scope for self-expression.

The never-married Miss Marple, of course, ran her own household with minor help, and thus would have been able to "retire" to rest and recollection without depriving any other family members of this required function of *listening*. Yet she did maintain many and varied connections in the world, and saw her duty as extending far beyond her own small household. Therefore this convention would have had some bearing on her need to retreat from others at times in order to reflect on how to knit up the strands of a difficult case.

As the narrator of *The Moving Finger* points out:

> It is a theory of mine that we owe most of our great inventions and most of the achievements of genius to idleness – either

enforced or voluntary. The human mind prefers to be spoon-fed with the thoughts of others, but deprived of such nourishment it will, reluctantly, begin to think for itself – and such thinking, remember, is original thinking and may have valuable results.

Miss Marple is often heard to be saying, while relating new data that is uncovered in the process of solving a crime: "If you'd just reflect a little – " (*Sleeping Murder*), and then retiring herself to go and do just that.

Jesus himself in the Gospels was often said to retreat to a quiet and sometimes deserted place to pray (Lk 5:16; 11:1). Out of the forty-day fasting retreat in the desert that preceded his active ministry (Mt 4:1–11), in which he overcame the most intense temptations Satan could throw at him, came the strength and resolve – the *vision* – that would carry him through to the Cross and beyond.

How can we assume that vision is so tied to healthy solitude? In Jesus' life as in those of his followers, it is by their *fruits* that their inner substance is confirmed. Melannie Svoboda has written in *Traits of a Healthy Spirituality* that:

> Jesus was always urging his disciples to 'study' life and thus to learn from it. Over and over again he exhorts his followers with words such as these: look, listen, take care, remember, watch, and pray – words that induce learning.

Much of this requires inner work.

The lessons are clear: *Stop. Reflect. Ponder. See.* There is danger in neglecting any of these steps, as Miss Marple informs Dolly Bantry in a conversation in *The Mirror Crack'd*. She cites the negative example of a mutual acquaintance, Alison Wilde: "She didn't know at all what the world was like. She didn't know what people were like. She'd never thought about them. And so, you see, she couldn't guard against things happening to her."

Movement back and forth, from solitude to community; from silence to engagement with the world. This is Jesus' pattern, and one that underlies both the way of Wisdom and of authentic discipleship for us all.

What can be expected of one who submits to the rigors of this pattern or life principle? *Great things*, but often manifested in small ways – in outcomes that matter to specific lives – in fact, that *restore* lives.

"She knows the things of old, and infers the things to come; she understands turns of speech and the solutions of riddles," the Apocryphal book *The Wisdom of Solomon* (8:8) says of the feminine figure Wisdom as teacher. She recognizes signs and discerns "the outcome of seasons and times."

Dr. Pender, an elderly clergyman in Agatha Christie's short story collection *The Tuesday Club Murders*, says in the first chapter: "Life itself is an unsolved mystery."

The "club" – which includes himself and Miss Marple, her nephew Raymond, and others – requires that each of the members relates a story-riddle from his or her past. Without revealing the outcome, they then encourage the others to 'solve' each mystery within the duration of the evening's gathering time.

Even here, in a situation in which her strengths will soon become evident, Miss Marple takes her time to respond.

"Aunt Jane, haven't you got anything to say?" her nephew asks.

"In a minute, dear," said Miss Marple. "I am afraid I have counted wrong. Two purl, three plain, slip one, two purl – yes, that's right. What did you say, dear?" [Perhaps she is 'buying' time.]

"What is your opinion?"

"You wouldn't like my opinion, dear," is her rejoinder. "Young people never do, I notice. It is better to say nothing."

And nothing is what she often says, when it is not yet the time to speak. In one story in this collection, *The Thumb Mark of St. Peter*, she reveals further how she goes about finding solutions to knotty problems:

> I was nearly at my wits' end, I can tell you. Now, I dare say you modern young people will laugh, but when I am in really bad trouble I always say a little prayer to myself – anywhere, when I am walking along a street, or at a bazaar. And I always get an answer. It may be some trifling thing, apparently quite unconnected with the subject, but there it is. I had that text pinned over my bed when I was a little girl: *Ask and you shall receive.* On the morning that I am telling you about, I was walking along the High Street, and I was praying hard. I shut my eyes, and when I opened them, what do you think I saw?

I won't give away the clue that enabled her to solve the case of an innocent woman accused of murdering her husband. But when Jane's nephew Raymond irreverently interjects: "An answer to prayer – a fresh haddock!" he is not far wrong.

As Miss Marple points out, "The hand of God is everywhere..." And perhaps only Miss Marple, outside the Gospels, could so felicitously connect the elements of faith and fish. But read the story.

Bede Griffiths, a British-born Indian Benedictine monk, has written:

> Contemplation unites us with God at a vertical level where we transcend ourselves, the world and all our problems, and experience oneness with God. It is at the same time a mode of action at the horizontal level by which we go out from the center of peace in God to the whole world. The further we go vertically towards God, the further we can go horizontally towards men. Jesus is the man who is totally given to God, to

the Father, the one who is totally surrendered to the vertical movement, so that the Son always sees what the Father is doing. At the same time he was totally open to all people and to life as a whole. That is the dual movement, vertical and horizontal, of contemplation in action, action in contemplation.

Thus is Miss Marple revealed to be both a *Mary* and a *Martha*, attending to her household and others' needs, but never neglecting the inner spiritual replenishment of relationship to God that makes it all possible.

But the practice of withdrawal, prayer, reflection, and then allowing puzzle pieces to fall into place does not imply a mystical solution. Jane Marple also reminds her listeners: "Has it ever occurred to you how much we go by what is called, I believe, the context?" She craves not only insight but exact evidence.

Intuition and the inner-hearing skills that are best developed in silence can push her in the right direction. But action and proof are always needed as well. Miss Marple once said: "A mediocre amount of intelligence is sometimes most dangerous. It does not take one far enough." Thus true focus and centeredness are always crucial to the process of interpreting the facts.

Yet she is never depicted as easily 'seeing' into the heart of the matter, whatever it might be, through some kind of spooky clairvoyance. Rather, she allows her cases' concrete facts to intermingle in her mind in much this fashion:

"I slept badly that night," recalls the narrator in *The Moving Finger*. "I think that, even then, there were pieces of the puzzle floating about in my mind. I believe that if I had given my mind to it, I could have solved the whole thing then and there. Otherwise, why did those fragments tag along so persistently?"

"Life is, after all, very much the same everywhere..." Miss Marple concludes in *Murder at the Vicarage*. Discerning the differences amid the sameness is part of her task.

Our efforts toward understanding and living the Christian life are not unlike this process. We are given guidelines, and the examples of others. We read Scripture and take the word into our hearts. But it is only over *time*, through engaging it and living it out, that a picture of God's purposes for us may finally come into focus.

Miss Marple herself is often grappling with a piece of a mystery just out of her reach. She needs time to allow fragments of evidence to gravitate toward the whole – until they can all fit into their proper places.

Yet through this process she doesn't think of herself as special. Drawing from all the different stories of people from St. Mary Mead that she remembers and recounts as examples to help her sort out new cases, she also affirms that: "Everybody is very much alike, really." *In our human weaknesses, our blind spots?* "But fortunately, perhaps, they don't realize it," she adds.

When the ex-Commissioner of Scotland Yard, Sir Henry Clithering, was staying in St. Mary Mead with his old friends Colonel and Mrs. Bantry (and before Dolly Bantry and Miss Marple became such close friends), Sir Henry asked them: "Tell me, do you know a Miss Marple?"

"Know Miss Marple? Who doesn't!" Dolly exclaims. "The typical old maid of fiction. Quite a dear, but hopelessly behind the times. Do you mean you would like me to ask *her* to dinner [as a sixth guest]?"

Sir Henry explains how he and five or six others had met regularly to propose mysterious stories and invite the others to use their deductive skill to see who could get nearest the truth.

"Like in the old story – we hardly realized," he tells them, "that Miss Marple was playing, but we were very polite about it – didn't want to harm the old dear's feelings. And now comes the cream of the jest. The old lady outdid us every time!" (from "The Blue Geranium").

Later, in the context of "The Four Suspects", another story in this early collection, Dr. Lloyd comments: "You're lost in a daydream, Miss Marple. What are you thinking out?"

Miss Marple gave a start.

"So stupid of me," she said [something she can never accurately be accused of]. And, to all their astonishment, she proceeds to contribute the exact key to solving the perplexing mystery of the evening.

In "A Christmas Tragedy", another mystery in *The Tuesday Club Murders*, Miss Marple reflects to the others:

What my nephew calls "superfluous women" have a lot of time on their hands, and their chief interest is usually *people*. And so, you see, they get to be what one might call *experts*. Now young people nowadays – they talk very freely about things that weren't mentioned in my young days, but on the other hand their minds are terribly innocent. They believe in everyone and everything. And if one tries to warn them, ever so gently, they tell one that one has a Victorian mind – and that, they say, is like a *sink*.

It is, perhaps, her fascinating "sink" of a mind that contains all that is needed for "propounding mysteries and giving solutions." She adds, "You were kind enough to say that I – that I did not do too badly," speaking up to Sir Henry.

"You beat us all," he answers warmly, nearer the end of the Tuesday night stories. "You displayed an absolute genius for getting to the truth."

The greatest mystery of all

Solitude is the place of purification.
– Martin Buber

Gail Godwin wrote in her nonfiction book *Heart: A Personal Journey Through Its Myths and Meanings*:

> The most revolutionary part of Jesus' teaching was that a good inner disposition – a good heart – is more important than following codes for correct external behavior. It's as simple as that, yet the literal-minded and the orthodox sticklers for form keep missing it. Where is this God's kingdom of yours, they keep asking him. What is it like? When is it coming? How should we behave to get in? Give us some rules. And he keeps telling them, it's here, it's all around you but you haven't recognized it, it's inside you, it's spread all over this earth, and the only rules you need worry about are loving God with your whole heart and loving one another as I have loved you.

Questions for Discussion:

1 How does Miss Marple exemplify the "good heart"? Which of her practices or skills in living this life impress you the most?

2 In what other ways does Miss Marple model the biblical ideal of being *a person for one's own times* – in truth, a prophet?

3 Describe the process through which God's will most commonly becomes revealed to you. How would you advise someone seeking to grow deeper in spiritual understanding?

4 What specific disciplines or practices have enabled you to enter into mature Christian life?

3

Who Is Our Neighbor?

A traveling businessman noticed the passenger seated next to him on a plane reading the Bible. During the flight, the two began talking. The businessman asked the gentleman which translation of the Bible he preferred. The passenger said he read the King James version because the lofty phrasing helped him feel closer to God. The businessman said that he preferred his grandmother's translation. The other man, familiar with many Bible translations, had never heard of a version translated by a grandmother, so he asked about it. The businessman replied, "Oh, her work was never put in writing; she translated the Bible into action every day of her life."
– William J. Parker, CSsR

I want you to be concerned about your next-door neighbor. Do you know your next-door neighbor... Each one of them is Jesus in disguise.
 – Mother Teresa

You cannot tell people what to do, you can only tell them parables; and that is what art really is, particular stories of particular people and experiences.
– W.H. Auden

An old rabbi once asked his pupils how he could tell when the night had ended and the day had begun. "Could it be," asked one student, "when you can see an animal in the distance and tell whether it's a sheep or a dog?"

"No," answered the rabbi.

Another asked, "Is it when you can look at a tree in the distance and tell whether it's a fig tree or a peach tree?"

"No," answered the rabbi.

"Then when is it?" the pupils demanded.

"It is when you can look on the face of any woman or man and see that it is your sister or brother. Because if you cannot see this, it is still night."

– Martin Buber in *Tales of the Hasidim*

If we are to take seriously the notion that charity begins 'at our own arm's reach', then we can find examples of it not only in the focus of Jesus' ministry toward crowds who implored him – but also in the responses to her neighbors of our fictional Christ-imitator Miss Marple.

Just as Jesus listened to people's problems and brought the wisdom of his Father to questions they had of *What is true?* and *How shall we act?* – so Miss Marple also considered her neighbors' well-being her responsibility, and put forth her best efforts to bring truth and peace to them in their confusing situations.

Jane Marple's nearest neighbors in the village of St. Mary Mead were Miss Hartnell and Miss Wetherby. Along with them, she is said to have made up "the old guard of ladies in reduced circumstances who lived in neat houses round the church." Her neighbors Colonel Arthur and Dolly Bantry were owners of a much grander home, a "good, solidly built" Victorian, Gossington Hall, the Colonel being the principal magistrate of the district. Dolly Bantry would become Miss Marple's close friend, and Miss Marple would come to her aid in helping solve the perplexing mystery of *The Body in the Library* of Gossington Hall.

She also becomes involved in the lives of many others of her neighbors, some who stay on in the other books, and a number who depart – not always in good graces.

But as Miss Marple's successes at solving crimes extended further and further in a wider circle and at various distant angles from the concerns of her small village, the question of *who is one's neighbor* – for whom does one 'stick out one's neck' – would be challenged. Still, the peculiar examples of people close to her, and their stories that bore witness to unpredictable village life, were always important references to turn back to and ruminate on in the midst of her later cases.

Who IS our neighbor? And why is determining this an excellent starting place for modeling Jesus' life? Jesus was once asked by a lawyer what he must do to inherit eternal life. The exchange takes on an adversarial tone as the lawyer seeks to test Jesus (Lk 10:25). In the give-and-take that follows, Jesus turns the question back on his questioner by asking the lawyer what the law or Torah has to say. The man responds with the "Summary of the Law" in Deuteronomy 6:5, *to love God*; and joins it to Leviticus 19:18, *to love one's neighbor* (cf. Mt 22:34–40; Mk 12:28–31). By combining the two commandments (v. 27), Jesus reveals them to be of equal importance. Jesus approves of the lawyer's answer, saying, "do this, and you will live" (v. 28).

Still the lawyer is not satisfied, and presses the point further as a way to 'justify' or further assert himself. "And who is my neighbor?" (v. 29), he asks. In other words, how shall I recognize the person I am obligated to love? This question derives from long-standing religious debates. And so, both to clarify and to expand the concept, Jesus tells a parable to let the listeners come up with an answer.

A Jewish man traveling to Jerusalem from Jericho was attacked by robbers, who stripped and beat him, leaving him half dead by the roadside. Traveling the road to Jerusalem was a high risk, so this was not unusual. Afterward three travelers came by. The first, a priest, passed by on the other side when he saw the injured man. Then when a Levite came down the road, he too avoided the man so as not to face ritual contamination from what appeared to be a dead body (Lev. 21:11).

The third traveler who came along was a Samaritan. There had been several centuries of conflict between Jews and

Samaritans (Jn 4:9), beginning with the Assyrian occupation in 722 BC. Samaritans had later opposed the rebuilding of the temple in Jerusalem, and worshiped at a shrine on Mt. Gerizim. Over the centuries other disputes over theology and liturgy ensued, and distrust led to diminished contact between the two groups.

So when the alien Samaritan came upon the injured traveler, he was "moved with pity" (v. 33) – indicating a strong empathy with the victim. In compassion, the Samaritan tended the man's wounds with oil and wine. Then he paid for the man's lodging at a nearby inn, promising to pay any additional costs on his return.

Jesus then asked which of the three travelers was a neighbor to the man who was attacked. When the lawyer replied, "The one who showed him mercy," Jesus told him to "go and do likewise" (Lk 10:37).

Miss Marple's spirituality, rooted in scriptural example and based on Christ's own life, requires her to do no less. Her even-handedness toward genuine needs of others around her is demonstrated again and again, as she seeks the truth for all, not favoritism for some. In *The Body in the Library*, she assists a 'shady' character that she believes to be involved, though she is sure that he is not the murderer. She suggests ways to support his innocence just before he is arrested.

"There is, as Miss Marple would say, a lot of human nature in all of us," as the Rev. Leonard Clement put it. And Miss Marple was not only quick to recognize this; she also had a vision for compassion that stretched beyond it.

Jeremy Waldron wrote in *The Monist* (July 2003):

The parable of the Good Samaritan first challenged an audience in an era where the road might still be seen as an exception: most people did live within the confines of community, and the morality of love for your neighbor was able to flourish in a context where your neighbor was likely to be someone just like you.

Yet today, even more so than in Miss Marple's day, as Waldron explains:

> We do not live in such an era. Much of our life is lived 'on the road', or lived in circumstances where we are often, in Kant's phrase, "unavoidably side-by-side" with strangers, with people alien to what we fancy are our traditions or our community. It may well be that a moral outlook that begins with the sheer fact of the proximity of two human beings – irrespective of their affiliations – is a better bet for these circumstances than a moral outlook which takes as its starting point what we owe to those we know and to those with whom we already have a connection.

Thus Waldron challenges us to be sensitive to the situations of those around us and to respond to them as though they were *all* our neighbors.

Theologian Helmut Thielicke perhaps answers the question best:

> Jesus' answer means simply, "You don't need any great specu-lation over the meaning of life; you just need to do the ordinary, everyday things; you need only be there when your fellow man is in difficulty, then you are already in accord with that meaning. Then you are not merely seeking that meaning; you are in the process of fulfilling it. For you will meet God himself in the imprisoned, the hungry, and the naked; when you are close to all of those, then you also dwell close to God, and you are in contact with the basic meaning and goal of your life."
> (in *How to Believe Again*)

There is no doubt in the Miss Marple stories that she consistently puts others' needs first, after humble assessment of her own situation and in sincere acceptance of her responsibility to live and act as Christ would have done.

In *The Mirror Crack'd* she would very much have liked to recall her former housekeeper, the Faithful Florence, to come care for her in her need again.

> But she [Florence] was at least sixty-five – perhaps more. And would she really want to be uprooted? She might accept that out of her very real devotion for Miss Marple. But did Miss Marple really want sacrifices made for her?

In the end she resolves to put these considerations for the well-being of another ahead of her own needs.

The circle of charity and Christian concern within which she lives is always a reminder of duty and a check of personal preferences. "In my own village, St. Mary Mead, things rather do revolve round the church," she once admitted.

Thus her close neighbors included the Rev. Leonard Clement (narrator of the first Miss Marple title, *The Murder at the Vicarage)* and his wife Griselda, who figures in several of the cases. Two other neighbors whose nearby cottages are mentioned in this first title were Mrs. Price Ridley and Dr. Haydock, physician and police surgeon. Other neighbors in this first description of the St. Mary Mead setting include artist Lawrence Redding and Mrs. Lestrange, along with several retired military men and their wives. Two other important people held titles of bank manager and solicitor – these more generic faces and names would change as time went on in the series.

But it is the character of Dolly Bantry who first challenges Miss Marple to radically attend to a neighbor's concerns, when a body is found one morning on the hearthrug in the library of her home with the Colonel, Gossington Hall, a large house in a parklike setting surrounded by woods.

A housemaid making her early morning rounds must awaken the master and mistress to announce that the body of an unknown young blonde woman has been found lying on the Bantrys' library floor.

Miss Marple's telephone rang when she was dressing. The sound of it flurried her a little. It was an unusual hour for her telephone to ring. So well ordered was her prim spinster's life that unforeseen telephone calls were a source of vivid conjecture. Nine o'clock to nine-thirty was the recognized time for the village to make friendly calls to neighbours. Plans for the day, invitations and so on were always issued then.

So the early call – at quarter to eight – was a bit perturbing.

It is revealed in the book that, after a call from the house to report the strange occurrence to the local police, Miss Marple was the next person alerted.

"Is that you, Jane?" Miss Marple was much surprised. "Yes, it's Jane. You're up very early, Dolly." Mrs. Bantry's voice came breathless and agitated over the wires… "We've just found a body in the library… She's just lying there in the library, dead. That's why you've got to come up at once."

"Of course, my dear, if you think I can be of any comfort to you – " Miss Marple answers.

Dolly Bantry returns: "Oh, I don't want comfort. But you're so good at bodies."

And although the most exciting cases do involve dead bodies, Miss Marple has also tended many ailing bodies in her time – perhaps as a war nurse, but certainly aiding the elder members of her own family before they passed on in death. Thus she learned to make hospital corners of the sheets, and recognized the skill when others had the ability to make them (sometimes providing a clue in itself).

Jane Marple plays down her early successes in this category of dead bodies as "mostly theoretical," but agrees at once to go help her friend Dolly "find out who did it and unravel the mystery and all that."

Her response is immediate: "Well, of course, my dear, if I can be of any *help* to you."

When the Chief Constable asks Colonel Bantry, "Hope your missus isn't too badly upset by it all?" he replies: "She's been wonderful – really wonderful. She's got old Miss Marple up here with her – from the village, you know." [Gossington Hall is about a mile and a half outside town.]

"Miss Marple?" The Chief Constable stiffened. "Why did she send for her?" "Oh, a woman wants another woman – don't you think so?"

Despite their doubts that the "old lady who knows everything that goes on in the village" and who has proved quite the local sleuth ["Put it over us properly once, didn't she?"] can do much: "She'll be out of her depth here"... nevertheless her loyalty and commitment to her friend put her generously 'on the spot' in this classic case.

By the time of the opening scene in *The Mirror Crack'd*, which comes chronologically nearly in the middle of the twelve Miss Marple novels, the village has changed following a second world war. Her neighbor Miss Hartnell was still alive, but Miss Wetherby had passed away and her house was inhabited by the bank manager and his family. Some of the houses had been given superficial renovations, so the little neighborhood looked much as before – except for the shops, which in Miss Marple's opinion showed "intemperate modernization."

But superficial changes, particularly the addition of a new housing development, bring fresh challenges and new opportunities to a woman committed to recognizing her neighbors even in sometimes unpleasant and disparate faces.

In *A Pocket Full of Rye*, Miss Marple becomes involved in investigating the poisoning death of businessman Mr. Rex Fortescue, who lives in Yew Tree Lodge in Baydon Heath, a newer development of homes for financiers who work "in the city." "Frankly, he was an odious man. Anybody might have done it," admits the housekeeper.

Miss Marple's mission is one of mercy and of duty, which becomes clear after the Fortescues' housemaid Gladys, whom Miss Marple herself once employed, becomes a victim as well.

"It's uncommonly good of you to have come here, Miss Marple," Inspector Neele was gracious when he saw "the mild, earnest face of the old lady" who had come to help solve the crime.

"It was my duty, Inspector Neele. The girl had lived in my house. I feel, in a sense, responsible for her. She was a very silly girl, you know."

Inspector Neele looked at her appreciatively and said: "Yes... just so."

"She had gone, he felt, to the heart of the matter."

And in *Sleeping Murder*, a young couple have bought a house in Dillmouth, a fictitious village on the south coast of Devon, that seemed perfect, but now is causing the young woman to experience déjà vu and a sense of unnatural dread about what might have occurred there decades ago. Miss Marple becomes involved in their investigations and urges them not to dig deeper and uncover things that might distress them further. But when they persist, she joins them in probing the past, even though she is feeling tired and run down.

Even "murder in retrospect... a horribly dangerous thing" when it is of importance to people she cares about must be attended to. And it is at the end of this book that Miss Marple does clearly risk her own life to save another's by second-guessing and confronting a murderer.

Miss Marple illustrates by example how wide our circle of neighbors reaches, when we are alert and attentive to duty, and sensitive to the finer promptings of conscience and intuition. She is never boastful or preachy about her successes, and often speaks in a downsized fashion about her own involvement, as though she only did what *any* Christian would not hesitate to do.

When the two solicitors tell her at the end of the mystery *Nemesis:* "It's been a splendid job, Miss Marple. We congratulate you," she answers simply and with great dignity, "Oh, well, it's just perseverance, isn't it, that leads to things?"

To persevere in consistency of character, expressing compassion and love-in-action surely is the best illustration of how one lives out an expanded definition of "who is our neighbor?" – and thus fulfills God's law of love.

Neighbors

God is a peacemaker, Jesus Christ is a peacemaker. So, if we want to be God's children and Christ's disciples, we must be peacemakers too.

The Christian life is not just our own private affair. If we have been born again into God's family, not only has he become our Father but every other Christian believer in the world, whatever his nation or denomination, has become our brother or sister in Christ.
– John Stott

The concept of war is outdated. Why? In the past, in some cases, it worked. In some cases the interest of one group and the interest of the other group were different, so the destruction of one group helped the other. But now, with the new global reality, the destruction of your neighbor means the destruction of yourself. Hence, using force to destroy your 'enemy' is now outdated. Therefore, out of respect and a genuine sense of their well-being, we have to find ways of reducing conflict. What is the best? Dialogue… First one must find peace with oneself, then with our family, then our neighbor, and finally, with our 'enemy'.

– The Dalai Lama, quoted in *Huffington Post*

Questions for Discussion:

1 Who do you believe is your neighbor or neighbors? How does this color the way you look at the world around you?

2 Why are love of God and love of neighbor so connected – indeed, each being essential to the other?

3 How does the example of Miss Marple in these stories expand your own idea of who is your neighbor?

4 We may not be called on to solve crimes as she was – but in what other ways can we bridge differences between family members, church members, neighborhood factions, and even national and international 'enemies'?

4

Truth Will Out

If one tells the truth one is sure sooner or later to be found out.
– Oscar Wilde

The moral arc of the universe is long, but it bends toward justice.
– Martin Luther King, Jr.

You can decide to take part in a plan you did not choose, doing things you do not know how to do for reasons you don't entirely understand. You can take part in a thrilling and dangerous scheme with no script and no guarantees. You can agree to smuggle God into the world inside your own body.
– Barbara Brown Taylor in *Gospel Medicine*

Jesus said that "If you continue in my word... you will know the truth, and the truth will make you free" (Jn 8:32). Jesus himself embodied the highest truth – living it, proclaiming it, calling others to its standards. For those who heed the call, it is possible to grow in becoming Jesus' light and justice in the world. But when individuals choose to oppose truth, the opposite of freedom results; they experience the stranglehold of deceit, and sometimes even death.

Miss Marple's creator herself, Agatha Christie, wrote that, "Truth, however bitter, can be accepted, and woven into a design for living." This is certainly true in the many mystery stories in which Miss Marple not only sides with truth, following her Christian conscience and sense of duty, but seems to *become one* with a drive for justice. Through her efforts, she herself becomes woven into the pattern that will eventually bring the case to a fair and just conclusion.

How does she do this? In the most personal and individual of ways: by being herself, a person with the highest ideals who prays, works, and, as much as possible, seeks to align her will with God's will.

She is not afraid to put strenuous demands on her own time, her personal energies, and her available resources. And she turns her decision-making faculties over to this force for good, as well.

In each story, it seems, something different is demanded of her; and even through doubts and many confusions, she rises to the occasion – not singlehandedly, but usually working within the specific community. She consistently relies on others around her as compatriots, to balance her, inform her, support her, and then to share in the credit when truth finally "outs."

"For all her fragile appearance, Miss Marple is capable of holding her own with any policeman or Chief Constable in existence," notes the vicar Leonard Clement in *The Murder at the Vicarage*. "Miss Marple is not the type of elderly lady who makes mistakes. She has got an uncanny knack of being always right." But she never expresses this inner certainty in an arrogant way – far from it – as she hides behind her knitting, her 'doddering' age, her "fluffy" appearance, and her awareness of men's frequent dismissal of women's contributions (and if the women are old and unremarkable looking, even of their *presence*).

How does she, with all of these liabilities, begin to work through the puzzles that present themselves to her? Not only does she have a 'nose' for truth, as some reporters are said to have for news; she can 'smell' a lie. For instance, in *A Caribbean Mystery*, when she notices that someone has said something less than true, she confronts him: "… It's the way you insisted on the point," said Miss Marple. "I have a certain experience of the way people tell lies."

In a discussion with other members of the group in *The Tuesday Club Murders* about crimes that go unpunished, Miss Marple comments on the fact that many crimes are never heard about and no one even knows they have been committed.

"I should think," said Miss Marple thoughtfully, "that there must be a very large number [of such cases]."

"Of course," she continues, "a lot of people are stupid. And stupid people get found out, whatever they do. But there are quite a number of people who aren't stupid, and one shudders to think of what they might accomplish unless they had very strongly rooted principles."

And again: "You say crime goes unpunished; but does it? Unpunished by the law perhaps; but cause and effect work outside the law. To say that every crime brings its own punishment is by way of being a platitude, and yet in my opinion nothing can be truer."

Truth will out. And it is possible to conclude that Miss Marple's aligning herself with Jesus' values, and desiring to "imitate" his way in the world, leads her to a holy vigilance. She is like an arrow pointed toward investigating and understanding anything and everything pertaining to a given case. And arguably, she herself demonstrates the 'incarnate' quality of truth: how it can be discovered; who lives and speaks it naturally; how to side with it and respect its predilection to prevail.

We have seen how, in order to facilitate the revelation of truth in the world, as Jesus did, she periodically withdraws to weigh her facts, sift evidence, and allow her mind to rise to a point that could be seen as *level* with the truth. But she also must mingle among other people and even seem to 'gossip' at times (and even to mislead as to her own intentions), in order to enable truth to out.

Murderers and other perpetrators take a real risk when they engage in any way with this woman who is nearly a stand-in for Truth; who, in the Wisdom phrasing of Psalm 1, has chosen "the way of the righteous." She does not follow the advice of the wicked, but allows the "streams" of goodness and compassion, a sense of fairness and also of intelligent discernment to nurture and guide her life.

"Murderers always find it difficult to keep things simple. They can't help themselves from elaborating," she observes, suggesting that one way to ferret out lies and subterfuges is to listen carefully to seemingly irrelevant details.

Oscar Wilde also once observed, "The truth is rarely pure and never simple." And as Agatha Christie wrote: "Crime is terribly revealing. Try and vary your methods as you will, your tastes, your habits, your attitude of mind, and your soul is revealed by your actions."

Through diligent sleuthing, the trademark touch or *modus operandi* of the perpetrator will often show up as a result of close examination of the facts. Christie put this comment in the mouth of her other famous detective Hercule Poirot in *The ABC Murders*:

There is nothing so dangerous for anyone who has something to hide as conversation! A human being, Hastings, cannot resist the opportunity to reveal himself and express his personality which conversation gives him. Every time he will give himself away.

Jesus himself frequently used the question and answer method in searching out the truth in the hearts of his listeners. We have seen how he used the Good Samaritan story to bring forth an answer to the important question of "Who is my neighbor?"

In the brief story of the two brothers in Matthew 21, a sort of abbreviated parable is related of a man who had two sons. He told the first son: "Go and work in the vineyard today." He answered, "I will not," but later changed his mind and went. The father told the second son the same thing, and he answered, "I go, Sir," but he did not go. Which of the two did the will of his father? (vv. 28–31). Which one embodied faithfulness?

Perhaps the simple conclusion can be drawn here that truth, like obedience, will ultimately be revealed not in what we *say* (or don't say), but in what we actually *do*. Certainly the biblical Wisdom approach calls us to pay attention to both.

At Jesus' triumphal entry into Jerusalem, his disciples are praising God and giving thanks for the deeds of power they have observed through him (Lk 19:37). When the Pharisees tell Jesus to order his followers to stop, he answers, "I tell you, if these were silent, the stones would shout out" (v. 40). If we as human souls do not bear witness to the truth, then he is saying that *something*, almost an organic entity or process, a 'truth wave', if you will, flows into the situation and reveals what is beneath the surface. *Truth will always out.*

Stories and parables, narrative and analogies are all potential vehicles in the subtle art of the uncovering of truth. Umberto Eco wrote in *Six Walks in the Fictional Woods*:

> By reading narrative, we escape the anxiety that attacks us when we try to say something about the world. This is the consoling function of narrative – the reason people tell stories, and have told stories from the beginning of time. And it has always been the paramount function of myth: to find a shape, a form, in the turmoil of human experience… I think that we read novels because they give us the comfortable sensation of living in worlds where the notion of truth is indisputable, while the actual world seems to be a more treacherous place.

This perspective helps account for the immense popularity of mysteries and detective novels, for instance, in which truth does prevail and criminals are caught and punished at the end. And everything is explained.

On a personal level, the lessons for the Christian life are

many. Mark Twain quipped that "If you tell the truth you don't have to remember anything." A bit of an exaggeration, but close to the "truth"! Personally siding with truth is simply a cleaner, less cluttered and more authentically human way to live. Not to mention, a Christian virtue.

In the stories, Miss Marple never assumes that the obvious explanation for a crime is the correct one. She realizes that very few people live by the ideal standard of absolute transparency toward God and others.

In *A Caribbean Mystery* we read:

This morning Miss Marple lay thinking soberly and constructively of murder, and what, if her suspicions were correct, she could do about it. It wasn't going to be easy. She had one weapon and one weapon only – and that was conversation. Old ladies were given to a good deal of rambling conversation. People were bored by this, but certainly did not suspect them of ulterior motives.

And so, as the little group around her spent the morning at the beach, she sat and seemed intent on her knitting. Her presence was quite unobtrusive and she only occasionally joined in the conversation – pure cover for her role as intelligent spy. When she *did* speak, everyone looked at her in surprise or sometimes indulgently – having forgotten she was even there.

In this novel, the path to truth had begun with a "gentle gesture of courtesy" on the part of Miss Marple, as she sat, the day before, listening to the boring Major Palgrave recount his "somewhat uninteresting recollections of a lifetime." Miss Marple, we are grateful to acknowledge, is herself only human. And so she found herself thinking her own thoughts, nodding as though in agreement so as not to hurt the old gentleman's feelings.

But as a result of her lack of attendance to certain points of continuity in the Major's stories, she soon fears a valuable clue might have been missed – after murder strikes within the small group of Caribbean seaside vacationers.

Later, when she is trying to extract information from the Major's kindly local doctor, she uses the excuse of an ailing knee to call on him (which she refers to by echoing the biblical phrase that her knee, like the poor, "was always with her"). This is mostly a ruse to gather information.

> Miss Marple had been brought up to have a proper regard for truth and was indeed by nature a very truthful person. But on certain occasions when she considered it her duty so to do, she could tell lies with a really astonishing verisimilitude.

In *They Do It with Mirrors* she allows an old friend to think she needs charity, in order to visit her under false pretenses to observe any danger the friend, Carrie Louise, may be in. It should be noted that in the few cases in which she misleads in order to obtain crucial information, she later 'comes clean' and reveals this as one of her methods for eliciting truths that can be justified for their importance in the saving of lives.

She was not afraid to strike a pose, either, as the "fluffy, pink-cheeked" spinster most people took her to be, or to ask an important question while feigning "a kind of dewy innocence." But if one were to look directly into her eyes, those "placid, china-blue" windows of her soul would undoubtedly have given her away as the shrewd discerner of truth that she was.

Even in the Caribbean setting that seemed an earthly paradise, "with its sunshine, its sea, its coral reef, its music," a virtual Garden of Eden, it is not surprising to find that there was the inevitable "shadow of the serpent" (again, Christie assumes her readers' awareness of biblical stories and symbols).

An offhand comment by the old Major might have been fabulous storytelling designed to impress. But *facts* speak volumes when it comes to ferreting out truth:

> "I don't know if I really believed him or not at the time," said Miss Marple. "But then, you see, the next day he died."
>
> "Yes," said Dr. Graham, struck by the clarity of that one sentence. *The next day he died...*"
>
> "And the snapshot had disappeared."

Miss Marple may seem to be living in a cosseted world of tea and gentle conversation and churchgoing and fetes. But it is clear in all the stories that in the world of other people and their fates, she is a key player. At one point she protests of the unsolved case, "I don't see how I can do anything about it – " But "she knew that she meant to try." Truth was too compelling a goal to sidestep or ignore even in the most difficult cases.

She is one who consistently regards the truth and the outing of it with utmost seriousness – as though her own life depends on it. Of course, she does not expect all of the clues to "fit" too neatly – "Who was she to demand Murders Made to Measure?"

"The truth is that one doesn't really know anything about anybody. Not even the people who are nearest to you ..." one character tellingly admits in *A Caribbean Mystery*. Yet Miss Marple had done a lot of listening in her life and was very skillful in tones of voice, as well as detecting lies. However, she sometimes confesses, "I've been stupid and a fool..."

At one point, "Miss Marple, feeling rather like a humble deputy of the Almighty, almost cried aloud her need in Biblical phrasing. *Who will go for me? Whom shall I send?* [echoing the call of the Prophet Isaiah]." Always the answer comes, and the situation usually calls for *her* to respond. In this instance the confidant who shows up at first demonstrates little outward respect for her, and "sounds like a man calling for his dog." Nevertheless, putting personal feelings aside, she is ready to align with another who is also seeking truth.

He is complimentary of her methods in a backhanded way: When she reminds him that he is rich and important, and people will take notice if *he* suggests something (while they would say she is an old lady imagining things), he answers:

They might at that. More fools if they did. I must say, though, that nobody would think you had any brains in your head to hear your usual line of talk. Actually, you've got a logical mind.

But much more than logic leads Miss Marple to her conclusions. As G.K. Chesterton wrote: "You can only find truth with logic if you have already found truth without it." Miss Marple's test of Truth rests on a deeper foundation than empirical evidence, as important as that is to her investigations.

"The trouble with you is that you're too conscientious," her partner in this mystery says, urging her to take a stand and not shilly-shally. But her innate sense of fairness and respect for other humans (while admitting their fallenness, and hers) requires her, as Jesus admonished, to "let the one who is without sin cast the first stone."

In short, Miss Marple's finely tuned conscience is involved at every level of her truth-seeking, and will not allow her to shortcut the process; cast doubts on the wrong (perhaps misunderstood) person(s); or precipitously rush to judgment. Her deeply held belief that "truth will out," that there is an almost organic process that could compel even *stones* to cry out, keeps her from being merely the busybody meddler that some authorities and rivals accuse her of being. "What I like about you," as Professor Wanstead tells her in *Nemesis*, "is your delightfully practical mind."

While her desire to imitate Christ in honest scrupulousness is clear in so many of the situations in these stories, she also manages to conform to the conventions of her society as a woman of her time. "Gentlemen, she knew, did not like to be put right in their facts." And she concedes: "It is never easy to repeat a conversation and be entirely accurate in what the other party to it has said." There are always tricky ambiguities to overcome before striking. She treads lightly; but always the light of truth beams out, as though from her very person.

"She had a lot of confused and contradictory ideas in her head, and… Miss Marple did not like… to have confused and contradictory ideas." In the end, truth DOES reveal itself within the satisfying parameters of *The Caribbean Mystery*. And as always, in these classic stories, therein lies the satisfaction of having struggled along with this very real, human, but sincerely Christian sleuth to get to the heart of truth and revelation that will set good people free.

Being caught by truth

The Bible teaches through story. When it wishes to express a profound truth, it shows us a person who represents that truth in the concrete reality of his or her life… Thus the story of his or her life becomes the story of every believer.
– Demetrius Dumm in *Flowers in the Desert: A Spirituality of the Bible*

From the cowardice that shrinks from new truth,
From the laziness that is content with half-truths,
From the arrogance that thinks it knows all truth,
O God of Truth, deliver us.
– Prayer of an ancient scholar

The truth is a snare: you cannot have it, without being caught. You cannot have the truth in such a way that you catch it, but only in such a way that it catches you.
– Søren Kierkegaard

Questions for Discussion:

1   What other impediments to the uncovering of truth can you name besides those mentioned in the prayer above: cowardice, laziness, and arrogance?

2   How can stories help us to understand truths that may elude us in our personal lives?

3   In what sense does the truth "catch" us, rather than our holding or having *it*? What are the implications in this for the way of Wisdom modeled by Miss Marple?

4   In what ways does the truth set you free?

5

Being Oneself Amid Imposters

Jesus asked his disciples, "Who do people say that the Son of Man is?" And they said, "Some say John the Baptist, but others Elijah, and still others Jeremiah or one of the prophets." He said to them, "But who do you say that I am?" Simon Peter answered, "You are the Messiah, the Son of the living God." – Matthew 16:13–16

A priest tells how he traveled to Africa to speak or teach or something of honor. An impoverished porter picked up his heavy and expensive suitcases and struggled toward the line of taxis. The priest was fuming that no one had met him at the airport, when the porter turned and introduced himself. He was the bishop.
   – Susan K. Bock

Watch for the opportune time, and beware of evil, and do not be ashamed to be yourself.
   – Sirach 4:20

After the Resurrection Jesus was recognized not by his outer qualities – he was never recognized by sight – but by his inner qualities, his Christ-self.
   – Madeleine L'Engle

It is never easy to stand up for Truth in this world of falsity and outright fallenness. Yet the call to be genuine, whole, and holy is an essential element in the imitation of Christ, especially as we seek to relate to others in a needy world.

In Miss Marple's world, as in Jesus' time and milieu, an authentic person not only stands out, but usually simultaneously *terrifies*, *attracts* and *confuses* others. It is so rare!

Even Jesus' disciples, who were the closest to him in his daily actions, his teachings, his indelible presence – were slow to grasp the fullness of who he was. In a world in which there were many voices of so-called prophets and would-be Messiahs, they were still capable of surprise and even shock, as when he stilled the storm on the sea, and they "were amazed, saying 'What sort of man is this, that even the winds and the sea obey him?'" (Mt 8:27).

Jesus challenged his followers themselves to be "salt" and "light" in a benighted world. In other words, they were to become the fullness of God-in-a-life that constituted their true call and vocation: to stand out, even to be misunderstood and persecuted, as he was.

Identifying with Truth, allowing it to seep out into the world through our very person, is always a serious business. And it requires not only a deep honesty with oneself but also a sense of being-with-God that seeks to emulate Jesus' own walk.

This path, of necessity, entails a certain humility of demeanor. Christ-imitators surely are the "meek" of Jesus' Beatitudes (Mt 5:1–11; cf. Lk 6:20–23), who in their quiet authenticity stand to "inherit the earth." It is a mystery, and counterintuitive to think of things in this way. It is almost as though the 'price tags' of all the world's qualities and values have been exactly turned around as to what people *think* are truly worthwhile, and those attributes they shun (such as humility) but ought to value.

What does it cost to "lose" oneself in this way in this world? The stakes are ultimate, Jesus says, with the loss and the gain being the same: everything. "Blessed are those who are persecuted for righteousness' sake, for theirs is the kingdom of heaven" (Mt 5:10). This is the ultimate price of authenticity, of standing with Truth – agreeing to share its destiny, even when Truth itself is on the "scaffold".

In the words of James Russell Lowell (1819–1891) in the poem/hymn *Once to Every Man and Nation*:

Though the cause of evil prosper,
yet the truth alone is strong;
Though her portion be the scaffold,
and upon the throne be wrong...

As Thomas à Kempis wrote in *The Imitation of Christ*: "If thou art willing to suffer no adversity, how wilt thou be the friend of Christ?" Identifying with Christ supplies both the impetus and the strength to *embrace truth* and share its destiny in our own particular circumstances, whatever they may be.

We have seen some instances already in which Miss Marple was prepared to do just that for the Truth: in her desire, quietly, dutifully, day by day to walk in Christ's way.

In the world of the Agatha Christie stories, we meet Miss Marple at some point between the two world wars (with *The Murder in the Vicarage*, first published in 1930). *The Moving Finger*, though set in the 1930s, wasn't published until 1942. Later stories seem to occur after the Second World War, though not much is revealed of Miss Marple's life during that wartime. But it is clearly after both wars that the novel *A Murder Is Announced* takes place (Agatha Christie's fiftieth work, published in 1950). Its plot makes use of the themes of wartime austerity and uncomfortable societal changes, including food and fuel shortages.

In this highly regarded book, as in a number of the Marple stories, one particular theme is important to the unfolding of the mystery. It is the phenomenon of mistaken identity, made possible by the number of misplaced persons, emigrants, and families separated following the wars. Often deliberate deceptions were perpetrated that allowed people to escape their pasts in a much easier fashion than one could today, now that we demand more accurate records, require more detailed legal paperwork, and sometimes even use DNA testing to prove identity.

"Fifteen years ago one knew who everybody was... But it's not like that anymore," Inspector Craddock observes regarding the changing of the old order in *A Murder Is Announced*. "Nobody knows anymore who anybody is."

Impersonation is a fruitful metaphor for subterfuge in general. It can entail neglecting one's responsibility, stealing another's good name, the license of anonymity, and sometimes the attempt to abscond with another's fortune, material or otherwise. The Miss Marple stories deal with false identity in various ways. Sometimes they involve a letter from the past in which the author is taken to be someone he or she isn't; or a supposed identification of someone in the present that turns out to be false, ploys that stand in for 'identity theft'. These misidentifications are just some of the varieties of falsity and pretense against which Miss Marple continually wars, seeking to counter deception in order to reveal identities.

The solution to one of the stories in *The Tuesday Club Murders* hinges on recognition of an insidious switched identity that allowed a woman literally to get away with murder and the stealing of a legacy. In order to sort out the confusing circumstances, Miss Marple refers to a case in St. Mary Mead of an old woman who successfully drew an old-age pension for three other women of neighboring parishes who were already dead.

When she introduces this example in the context of solving that particular Tuesday night crime, Sir Henry Clithering at first protests, "But it doesn't seem to me to throw any light upon our present problem."

"Of course not," said Miss Marple. "It wouldn't – to you. But some of the families were very poor, and the old age pension was a great boon to the children... But what I really meant was that the whole thing hinged upon one old woman being so like any other old woman."

In this case that they are solving in a drawing-room fashion, the two women described in the story are on vacation together, and no one around them much distinguishes between them.

After one of the women is "accidentally" drowned, why would people NOT believe the surviving woman to be who she claimed to be?

Clearly, it is a wicked world of deception in which people's true agendas are often cleverly disguised. Certainly not everyone has Miss Marple's integrity of personhood. She is humble and self-effacing in the stories, sometimes to the point of fading into near-invisibility. Yet all of this also enables her detective craft and adds to her success in rooting out evil. *Who she is*, a woman for others embodying humility and servanthood, can be found in every facet of her remarkable life revealed on these pages.

"Remember that an elderly unmarried woman who knits and gardens is streets ahead of any detective sergeant. She can tell you what might have happened and what ought to have happened and even what actually did happen. And she can tell you why it happened!" is how Sir Henry described her to his nephew Inspector Craddock of Scotland Yard (in *A Murder Is Announced*).

Authentically being oneself is also a quality that Miss Marple appreciates in others. When a person or witness can be believed, and has the transparent qualities required of being truly Christian in the world, much is gained in time and energy that can be applied toward facilitating good from the get-go.

In *The Moving Finger*, Miss Marple notes, "Mrs. Dane Calthrop is a very remarkable woman, you know. She's nearly always right." The narrator answers, "It makes her rather alarming." To which Miss Marple responds, "Sincerity has that effect." And, she believes, "It's not a man's birth that matters, but what he *is*."

Thus, surely, sincerity of personhood can be considered truly akin to godliness. As Thomas à Kempis wrote in *The Inner Life*:

A sure way of retaining the grace of heaven is to disregard outward appearances, and diligently to cultivate such things as foster amendment of life and fervour of soul, rather than to cultivate those qualities that seem most popular.

Yet being oneself, for us humans, does not mean always being right. Rami Shapiro writes of the way of Wisdom in his commentary in *The Divine Feminine in Biblical Wisdom Literature*:

> Everyone makes mistakes, follows dead ends, and takes detours that promise much and yield nothing. If you imagine that making these mistakes precludes you from changing course, then your imagination has doomed you. If you realize, however, that you are never lost as long as your eye remains fixed on the goal, then you will allow for error and the shame error sometimes carries; you will feel the shame and move beyond it.

He translates the Wisdom of Jesus ben Sirach 4:20-21 as:

> Act harmoniously with each moment, beware of evil, and do not fear shame. There is a false shame that leads to error, but there is a true shame that leads to grace.

Surely Miss Marple, through the trial and error method of her amateur sleuthing, knows and exhibits this grace again and again, in book after book.

It is indisputable that those who insist on being imposters for their own material gain, at the expense of their souls, *can* be highly successful in the short term, since, as Miss Marple notes, "In essence... people are highly credulous." Novelist Peter Tremayne wrote in his mystery *Shroud for the Archbishop*, "Most of the harm done in this world is due to people who want to feel important and set about trying to impress their importance on others." And it usually works, for a time.

And, in the course of the plots, even Miss Marple herself sometimes is expected to 'play a role' that hides her deeper critical faculties and inner spiritual depth. At one point Inspector Craddock warns her not to snoop around, as they are investigating in *A Murder Is Announced*. He has a feeling it isn't *safe*. She answers:

> "But I'm afraid that we old women always do snoop. It would be very odd and much more noticeable if I didn't. Questions about mutual friends in different parts of the world and whether they remember so and so, and do they remember who it was that Lady Somebody's daughter married? All that helps, doesn't it?"

"Helps?" asks the Inspector, not 'getting it'. "Helps to find out if people are who they say they are," said Miss Marple. As a true person at one with herself, she knows how to recognize lies about identity. And, she observes in *They Do It with Mirrors*, "so few people ever did look like what they really were."

Miss Marple knows who she is. She may sometimes even exaggerate if necessary to maintain the credibility she needs to keep probing, keep hollowing out the space for the truth to fill in and reveal itself naturally: "I'm only too delighted to be of use in any way. At my age, you know, one feels very useless in the world," she once humbly remarked.

Though we don't know a great deal about Miss Marple's earlier life, not to mention exactly what she did during the wars, it is revealed at times that she has had a long, dutiful experience of nursing others in need. Being old, she seems to have survived everyone else in her family, including her one sister (whom she never names or writes about, but whose children and grandchildren are those she knits for: great-nephews and nieces that she dotes on).

Once in her youth, we read in *A Caribbean Mystery*, she had met a potential suitor at a croquet party, who ultimately revealed himself to be dull and thus undesirable. He had seemed exciting and a bit of a "Bohemian", which would have attracted her above-average mind and fed into her creativity. But when her father took to him too quickly, she recognized the young man to be boring after all. She apparently never regretted the loss of this marriage opportunity.

The path of determining *who one really is* is a lifetime process. For the Christian, it can be seen as analogous to one's walk with Christ, through trials, toward spiritual maturity. The Apostle Paul wrote in 1 Corinthians 13:12–13:

> For now we see in a mirror, dimly, but then we will see face to face. Now I know only in part; then I will know fully, even as I have been fully known. And now faith, hope, and love abide, these three; and the greatest of these is love.

And herein is the key to living consistently as *who we are*, what we know to be the Truth, and what we aspire to be included in, reflecting Christ: Love itself.

Thomas Merton wrote:

> If we attempt to act and do things for others or for the world without deepening our own self-understanding, our own freedom, integrity and capacity to love, we will not have anything to give to others. We will communicate nothing but the contagion of our own obsessions, our aggressiveness, our own ego-centered ambitions.

And so, for me, these stories of detection, discovery, and deliverance from falsity and evil also seem to carry the underlying plotline of a soul's development among other souls. For even as the character of Miss Marple grows and rises to new occasions, she is not above learning from her circumstances something concerning *herself* as well as about the nature of good and evil in the world.

The arc of Miss Marple's inner development, the following of her own progress in the Christ-life, as well as charting its effect on those around her, can be described as almost a second narrative in the books.

Joseph Campbell wrote: "Spiritual life is the bouquet, the perfume, the flowering and fulfillment of a human life, not a supernatural virtue imposed on it." This is the way it appears from the outside, as we evaluate a life such as Mother Teresa's, for instance, or Miss Marple's – and even, in a mystery, Christ's own human fulfillment of his mission in earthly terms and time.

But *to the soul*, from the inside, such a flowering is experienced instead as a supernatural receiving, from God's fullness in Christ, the gift of "grace upon grace" (Jn 1:14). And this receiving is always to be followed up by reciprocal self-offering: "Give, and it will be given to you," we are told. "A good measure, pressed down, shaken together, running over, will be put into your lap; for the measure you give will be the measure you get back" (Lk 6:38).

This is the rule by which Miss Marple lives in her life as a true self among others who may not hold to her stringent standards. But she is overall unwavering in her life as a woman for others who stands *for* and *with* the Truth: simply as herself.

Spiritual life as gift and habit

In all faces the Face of faces is veiled as a riddle.
– Nicholas of Cusa (15th c. Christian mystic)

How does peace come? Simple. By accepting who we are and what we have as enough for us. By recognizing and respecting who the other is and what they have as theirs. By finding within ourselves "the pearl of great price," the richest thing there is in life, the sense of the presence of the God who loves and companions us through all the pressures of life. "In moderating, not in satisfying, desires," Reginald Heber wrote, "lies peace." Then we find that we have changed... Then we begin to dedicate ourselves to that highest possible level of humanity that not only does good but, most of all, does no harm... To do no harm... requires real care, genuine compassion, true realization that the glow of the other diminishes no glow of my own. Then my own life begins to shine even more.

– Sr. Joan Chittister in *Uncommon Gratitude: Alleluia for All That Is*

Questions for Discussion:

1 How would you describe the flowering of your own spiritual life as both gift and human process? How much do we ourselves contribute and what amount is God's bestowed grace of vocation and subsequent guidance?

2 How does this tension relate to the whole question of God's providence and our free will to respond? What lessons can we gain from Christ's life in this regard?

3 What are the common signs of authenticity of personhood that you observe in those around you? Why does being oneself in the world matter so much?

4 How does the example of Miss Marple in these stories reveal to you ways that *being* or *becoming* your own authentic self is key to a fruitful Christian life?

6

The Easy Chair, the Garden Path, and the Wicked World

Men don't believe in the devil now, as their fathers used to do.

They've forced the door of the broadest creed to let his majesty through;

there isn't a print of his cloven foot, or a fiery dart from his brow,

to be found in the earth or air today, for the world has voted so.

But who is mixing the fatal draught that palsies heart and brain,

and loads the earth of each passing year with ten hundred thousand slain?

Who blights the bloom of the land today with the fiery breath of hell,

if the devil isn't and never was? Won't somebody rise and tell?

Who dogs the steps of the toiling saint, and digs the pits for his feet?

Who sows the tares in the field of Time wherever God sows his wheat?

The devil is voted not to be, and of course the thing is true;

but who is doing the kind of work the devil alone should do?

We are told he does not go about as a roaring lion now.

But whom shall we hold responsible for the everlasting row

to be heard in home, in church, in state, to the earth's remotest bound,

if the devil, by a unanimous vote, is nowhere to be found?

Won't somebody step to the front forthwith and make his bow and show

how the frauds and crime of the day spring up, for surely we want to know.

The devil was fairly voted out, and of course the devil's gone;

but simple people would like to know who carries his business on.

– Author unknown

"There is a great deal of wickedness in village life. I hope you dear young people will never realize how very wicked the world is."
– Miss Marple in "The Blood-Stained Pavement"

If one is to do good, it must be done in minute particulars.
– William Blake

If it seems a stretch to imagine the prim and self-contained Miss Marple, with a puzzled brow, sitting in her drawing room ruminating over a case, as God's champion in the world – we need to remember that, as Mother Teresa said, "We can do no great things, only small things with great love."

Miss Marple's ministrations, sometimes from the comfort of an easy chair in which she knits and *listens*, may seem small and inconsequential in a world of evil machinations and innocent people being led down "the garden path". But enjoying padded chairs and the pleasures of gardening are positive qualities (and reasonable tools) in her quest to root out evil whenever she encounters it.

Miss Marple's goodness certainly shines out in the books in which she stars, as she puts other people ahead of her own interests time after time. Having intentionally aligned herself with the Truth, in imitation of Christ, she seeks ways to act through her own physical situation, gifts, and natural limitations, allowing for revelations that will free the innocent.

Miss Marple has "had a long life of experience in noticing evil..." we read in *At Bertram's Hotel*. "The arm-chairs in this hotel have very high backs. Very comfortable they are. I was sitting in one of them," she admits. "I suppose you didn't realize there was anyone else in the room..." Such is a typical situation in which a mostly sedentary, but dauntingly perceptive detective is able to do her part.

She is an elderly woman who tends her small cottage with minimal outside help, who keeps a pair of binoculars handy (with the excuse of a bird-watching hobby) to extend her vision when needed: to observe what the neighbors are really about, especially when something seems curious or "not quite right".

Miss Marple has seen wickedness both close up and in the world at large, and is far from naïve about what might be going on, even in the highest circles of society. And though she makes an effort to be charitable in her assessment of people, experience has taught her not to automatically give the questionable ones the benefit of the doubt. Rather, "she invariably thought the worst, and nine times out of ten, so she insisted, she was right in doing so." She also finds other people highly credulous – ready to believe what they are told whole cloth – a weakness which can also enable and perpetuate evil.

"Her nephew had once compared life in St. Mary Mead to scum on a pond, and she had indignantly pointed out that smeared on a slide under the microscope there would be plenty of life to be observed" (from *A Caribbean Mystery*). And there is always, in the stories, plenty of scum to go around!

But there is also a certain sadness in this necessarily jaded evaluation of other people and their motives, and in her credulity as to what lengths they are capable of. Miss Marple takes the doctrine of the fallenness of creation seriously, as when she once referred to the "shadow of the serpent" over an idyllic scene. However, she affirms that: "One always has *hope* for human nature." And she seeks to restore order and peace through whatever small actions and solutions she can send forth into the world, from the place where she is contentedly 'planted'.

The garden that she maintains outside her cottage in St. Mary Mead is a vital key to her innate understanding of the cycles of life. She is sadly cognizant of how, as in the biblical parable, the wheat and the "tares" or weeds grow up together and sometimes can't be sorted out right away. If the weeds are precipitously rooted out then the good plants around them can be bruised or destroyed, as in Jesus' teaching. And in the process of pruning, even greater evil can be unleashed. Even when she is fairly certain who a perpetrator is, she will not tell someone like Dolly Bantry, who begs her to reveal it. She knows that Dolly can't keep her mouth shut and could thwart the slow and painstakingly verified path to justice.

The "easy chair" and Miss Marple's sitting, knitting, and observing are more than a backdrop or a cover for this highly effective garden sleuth. They are also useful occupations that can foster serious reflection and serve to *give her time*. As Ecclesiastes 9:10 admonishes: "What your hand finds to do… do with all your might." And she is also clearly following the advice of George Washington to "Labor to keep alive in your breast that little spark of celestial fire, called conscience."

In *The Mirror Crack'd* Miss Marple's doctor suggests that, since she is always dropping stitches, she consider *unraveling* rather than knitting for awhile, an action parallel to unraveling the murder – and she takes his advice. The literarily aware reader is meant to make the connection to Penelope, Odysseus' faithful wife in Homer's classic *The Odyssey*. Penelope was able to 'buy' time by unraveling the knitting of her father-in-law's shroud; undoing her day's work every night rather than trying to make unimpeded progress.

Though the situation is quite different, the same principle applies. In the absence of her husband, Penelope was besieged by many suitors. But she managed to put off choosing who would replace her husband in the event of his not coming back from his travels. She did this by asserting that she would not choose a new husband until she had finished weaving a shroud for Odysseus' father Laertes. But for three years she would weave during the day and then unravel her work at night, so that no complete handiwork ensued. And thus she 'gained' time, the most precious commodity to the wise woman in learning how to live rightly. This wonderful metaphor highlights a feminine quality of working within limits *to arrange for good* the pieces of reality to which she has access.

This womanly wisdom is certainly in the spirit of Herman Hesse's thought that "Whether you and I and a few others will renew the world some day remains to be seen. But within ourselves we must renew it each day."

Against what evil must the world be protected and renewed for good? Sometimes a seemingly small sin of greed or pride or lust lurks behind an entire chain reaction resulting in an outpouring of evil. And just as Miss Marple unravels her own handiwork, as a detective she traces the thread back to the beginning where evil might just be explained – and sometimes thwarted – in time. Or course, at other times it is too late to save those she seeks to protect. But whenever and to whatever extent knowledge is released and truth revealed, some saving value will be realized.

Miss Marple once remarked (in *The Tuesday Club Murders*) that "A mediocre amount of intelligence is sometimes most dangerous. It does not take one far enough." And T.H. Huxley asked, "If a little knowledge is dangerous, where is the man [or woman?] who has so much as to be out of danger?" In Miss Marple we come close to an answer.

Very often Miss Marple's success depends upon 'kitchen variety' knowledge, intelligence earned and practiced in the most seemingly mundane activities of her quiet spinsterly life. For instance, in "The Four Suspects", a story in the collection *The Tuesday Club Murders*, her acquaintance with the technical names for certain garden flowers, gained from yearly perusing of seasonal plant catalogs, proves crucial. This knowledge clues her in to the meaning of a cryptic message in which these names are alluded to, enabling her to identify the guilty and eliminate the innocent from suspicion.

In *At Bertram's Hotel* she also employs a garden metaphor to help solve a puzzle of deception. She explains: "It is like when you get ground elder really badly in a border. There's nothing else you can do about it – except dig the whole thing up." Her companion in sleuthing replies: "I don't know much about gardens. But change the metaphor to dry rot and I'd agree." And of course, they are both right.

There is no telling where evil may turn up next. In Agatha Christie's foreword to her second full-length Miss Marple mystery, *The Body in the Library*, the author writes: "I laid down for myself certain conditions. The library in question must be a highly orthodox and conventional library. The body, on the other hand, must be a wildly improbable and highly sensational body." Wickedness sometimes protrudes in the form of a garish murder: on the stairs or in a lane, in the night or in between breakfast and tea. We inhabit a world in which anything can happen to anyone, no matter how improbable. And so even the wildest conjectures as to how the "serpent" might have insinuated his presence into the garden must be considered. All of this makes Christie's mysteries both classic and individually unique. And finding the truth is never simple; for Miss Marple, "The children of Lucifer are often beautiful" – and unlikely. As Agatha Christie wrote: "Evil is not something superhuman, it's something less than human."

But the combating of it requires the best that humans themselves can conscientiously do, *with God's help* (which Miss Marple unmistakably implores from time to time). Her presence in and among the intertwined good and evil of life leads to the question: How can our simple actions for and against each other result in such large consequences in the world? Each story follows that thread back to the beginning to offer an answer. And Miss Marple's own example illustrates graphically that it is only by acting *from our own center*, authentically, *for the good itself and not our own gain*, that evil is combated – though never fully vanquished.

"Miss Marple... read a few verses of the Thomas à Kempis which she kept by her bed, then she turned out the light. In the darkness she sent up a prayer. One couldn't do everything oneself. One had to have help," we read in *A Caribbean Mystery*.

Julian of Norwich tells us: "God did not say: You will not be troubled, you will not be be-labored, you will not be disquieted; but he said: You will not be overcome. God wants us to pay attention to these words, and always to be strong in faithful trust, in well and woe."

I remember a sort of 'Miss Marple' I encountered once, though only recently have I thought to make the connection. This older woman both voiced and stood up singly for the Truth in a situation in which several other people were being duped by a colleague of hers and theirs. She did it at great risk to her own job and perhaps even her safety. As with Miss Marple's selfless venturing outside the 'comfort zone' of her cozy cottage, garden, and neighborhood into the wicked world, the friend I'll call Linda boldly confronted the perpetrator to his face. Her courage caused a chain reaction of discovery and eventually brought about a certain level of justice. And she was able to keep her job, a miracle in itself, but one that was by no means certain from the outset.

Combating evil from her easy chair is nevertheless uncharted territory for Miss Marple in each case she takes on. And always the effort leads her beyond that comfortable setting into the precincts of danger. Though we do not have maps to get us through the 'dark woods' that lie along the borders of our safe homes and situations, yet we also must venture out when duty requires it of us. And just as Miss Marple found inspiration from her nightly reading of *The Imitation of Christ*, we too have the examples of biblical figures and saints through the ages who risked greatly for love – and who found the reward of such ethical, Christlike living to be priceless treasure.

Each person who takes on the task of countering evil, in whatever way is possible in his or her individual life, is walking in the way of Christ. And in this manner we are called to participate in his redemptive acts that continue in the "wicked world" today. Each sedentary, contemplative (or active) saint will in a sense thereby become one with us, sharing our humanity as we all seek to follow 'in his steps'.

The treasure of each other

Megan McKenna writes in her book *Parables: The Arrows of God* about the parable of "the treasure in the field". It tells of a man who sells all that he has to buy a piece of land so that he may uncover and own the wealth that is buried in it. McKenna admonishes:

> "We can't just take the treasure for ourselves without community, without the world and the fact that we are responsible for each other... The kingdom is all of our relationships with God seen and known by others outside the community as well as by those within the believing group. So that is the treasure. What of the field? The field is where the relationship is expressed, among people. The field is where we return the treasure we found. We hide it again, sell all that we have and go back and buy the field – move in with the folk. What does this mean?... Even holiness has to be done together. This is a dream, the dream of God."

McKenna concludes:

> The treasure is hidden in the field. The incarnation is hidden in people and in their needs and sorrows and hopes. Together the treasure is shared in the field. We are supposed to become the treasure hidden in the field, a new reality in the world, along with Jesus, and anyone who stumbles upon us will rejoice exceedingly and go therefore and sell everything they have to come back to the field, to us, and share the treasure.

Teresa de Jesus tells us:

> The important thing is not to think much but to love much and so do that which best stirs you to love. Love is not great delight, but desire to please God in everything.

Questions for Discussion:

1 How would you define the "treasure" of community responsibility in Christ? What has it required of you personally?

2 How does the particularity of Miss Marple's situation enlarge your imagination as to how to harness quotidian tasks and gifts for the Kingdom?

3 What determines how you view the world? What has been your reaction to the mixed clues of your daily life? Do you frequently see them as a challenge, as a threat, or as opportunity?

4 How does Scripture prepare us to encounter and challenge the evil around us? What gifts have you been given that enable your own contribution to the process?

7

Deciphering the Reality Behind Appearances

"I see that you are that favorite character of fiction, the amateur detective. I don't know that they really hold their own with the professional in real life."
– The Rev. Leonard Clement in *The Murder at the Vicarage*

Treat no one lightly and think nothing is useless, for everyone has a moment and everything has its place.
– Ben Azzai

"Pigs may fly, but they're very unlikely birds."
– A saying of Miss Marple's grandmother

It's somewhat daunting to reflect that Hell is – possibly – the place where you are stuck in your own personal narrative forever, and Heaven is – possibly – the place where you can ditch it, and take up wisdom instead.
– Margaret Atwood in *Negotiating with the Dead*

The Apostle Paul admonished us to "Be transformed by the renewing of your minds" (Rom 12:2). It is a challenge to consider that, even when we think we are on the right track with our lives, aligned with truth as we perceive it, and seeking to bring about good – we will always have deficits of understanding that need renewing, reforming, refreshing in order to come to yet deeper levels of comprehension and insight.

The authenticity of Christ challenges us also to live in honesty and transparency – to be truly ourselves among others, that close and extended field of other humans that are all in some sense our 'neighbors'. For the Christian, it should mean an ever widening, ever deepening journey, such that the things we thought we understood in the past are now to us like "milk". They might have gotten us to where we are, but now we will need stronger, more nourishing fare, the "meat" of Wisdom (cf. Hebrews 5:13–14).

In John 2:23 the Evangelist reports that many believed in Jesus because they saw the signs that he was doing. "But Jesus on his part would not entrust himself to them, because he knew all people and needed no one to testify about anyone; for he himself knew what was in everyone" (v. 24). Jesus saw through to the heart within, regardless of people's words and appearances. And he dealt with souls in their various needs and degrees of comprehension, on whatever level they were able to hear him.

We too must operate in the world in this way. We must learn to discern and implement practical wisdom within *context*. We have seen how being oneself among various imposters positions Miss Marple (and ourselves) in regard to the authentic *being* that Jesus possessed. Yet there is always more to uncover: broader circumstances that surround any situation; facts which *seem* to point one way, but may indicate underlying puzzles or have alternate meanings. Ferreting out honest answers and determining how to act in life's dilemmas will require a probing intellect and a selfless spirit, as well as true compassion for those around us who suffer from the world's falsity and deception.

In *At Bertram's Hotel*, Miss Marple has returned to a luxurious vacation spot that had meant something to her in her youth. One character describes Bertram's Hotel as "a wonderful place in London... It's just like stepping back a hundred years. It just *is* old England! And the people who stay there! People you'd never come across anywhere else... All the old English dishes... And it's wonderfully comfortable. And warm. Great log fires." Who wouldn't want to experience a return visit to such an idyllic place, even (nearly) sixty years later (as Miss Marple does)?

But just as Miss Marple is adept at uncovering imposters, so her authenticity meter is accurate and alerts her (she once had an aunt who could "smell" lies) in regard to places and situations. She astutely observes of Bertram's Hotel: "Behind the appearances, things might be very different."

With Miss Marple, surface observations and inner prognostications – or at least educated 'hunches' – are always going on at the same time on different levels. She is not a hardened cynic who sneers at comments people make or questions motives outwardly. Her frequent, sober comment when an unpleasant controversy is posed to her in conversation might be the empathetic, "I'm sure it is all a most difficult problem."

Her Christian charity and naturally thoughtful disposition make her the perfect guest at country house or gala event or unusual vacation spot, or simply among small gatherings of neighbors in St. Mary Mead. But always her eagle eye and innate curiosity, combined with an ability to ascertain true character, combine to give her an edge.

She is quick and perceptive in her discernment of what is REALLY going on – not prone to precipitous conclusion, but working toward her answers through a slow and deliberate process. Having the patience of Penelope, she can allow everything to move into its correct place, gradually revealing to her its lines of delineation, as though an enigma were organically solving itself.

She begins from a view of human nature that always takes into account the fact that temptation is ever present to humans. There is also the factor that people in general are weak, especially when their higher nature is not being supported through habitual discipline and perpetual vigilance. "I always find it prudent to suspect everybody just a little," she has said. For her, it is no mystery that weeds will always grow up amid healthy plants.

Jesus in his ministry frequently told nature- and life-based parables that compared physical phenomena to the spiritual conditions of souls. In the Parable of the Sower, which is found in all three synoptic Gospels, he spoke of the word being spread abroad, with some seeds falling by the wayside, and some falling on stony ground without enough soil to grow in (springing up, but with no depth). Others fell among thorns that choked out their life. But still others landed on good ground, and in their time increased in strength to bring forth impressive fruit (Mt 13:3–23).

Each landing place of the various seed represented a type of soul or circumstance that determined its fate. Poet Rainer Maria Rilke sheds this light on the mysterious process of how we become who we are: "That which we call destiny goes forth from within people, not from without into them." Perhaps the conditions of our soul/soil from the beginning have a great deal to do with how we will "land" among others in the field of life.

In the parable, the seed that falls by the wayside is simply borne away by 'Satan' or temptations to doubt; the seed in stony ground represents those of facile belief whose lives do not withstand testing; the seed among thorns likewise are choked out by circumstances, temptations, overindulgences, and other elements that war with truth.

The seed (in the parable, the word) that falls on good ground eventually becomes revealed for what it was. And in the case of souls, their character becomes unveiled in much the same way, *over time*. These are people who have aligned themselves with the Truth, who stand by their word and choose the good, even when challenged by confusing doubts and tests.

Fritz Kunkel wrote in *Creation Continues*:

The problem, of course, is not the understanding of the four groups of hearers; it is the understanding of our own inner situation. If our mind is a stony place, our only concern is to rid ourselves of the stones. The simple question, "What are the stones in our soul?" may start a self-analysis which will occupy us for weeks and lead to extremely disagreeable though helpful discoveries...

If we decide that thorns are in the way we will have to clear the soil, like pioneers who settle in a new land; and if our soul is like the wayside, we simply have to plow and build a new path skirting the field. In all three cases the soil can be prepared by human effort... There is no end to the discoveries if the creative meditation has been started by the first vague hearing of the word.

There are subtleties regarding souls *and* circumstances laced throughout the Miss Marple stories. And, as always, author Agatha Christie has included numerous 'red herrings': characters who seem possibly guilty or have other secrets they are hiding; situations that appear damning on the surface but may obscure complicated relationships and hide underlying facts that the reader is not privy to; ambiguities such as whether a suspected cause of death was the actual means used, and doubts concerning timing and motive.

Agatha Christie admits she was especially fond of poisoning deaths in her stories. But even this plot device is not always straightforward. As Paracelsus wrote: "All things are poisons, for there is nothing without poisonous qualities. It is only the dose which makes a thing poison." Appearances can deceive.

Facades and distracting superficial confusions abound. And in actuality, usually there is only one line of connection between cause of death and perpetrator (though even in this the clever author sometimes confounds simple logic when the final unraveling of a case is revealed). Tracing the one thread back to the spool from which it came is as much an art as creating a plan from whole cloth. Thus the genius of the writer is revealed, and Miss Marple's prowess celebrated.

Christie seems to take pleasure in illustrating characters who embody hypocrisy, as in Ambrose Bierce's definition of the word 'mausoleum' in *The Devil's Dictionary*: "(n) The final and funniest folly of the rich." Many a pompous character gets his or her just deserts in these satisfying tales.

Even "healthy plants", or characters that seem to be thriving, often can be shown to be shallow individuals barely rooted in surface soil, who will collapse under police interrogation aided by the careful sleuthing of Miss Marple. Surprises abound. "Those quiet ones are often the worst. Jane Marple says so," observes her neighbor Miss Wetherby in *The Body in the Library*.

How has Miss Marple become so adept at discerning the meaning of a situation beyond its appearances? She herself has learned the lifelong practice of conscientiousness: "the qualities of a prudent, persistent, well-organized person," as noted in a *Slate* article by Emily Yoffe. In "Don't Stop Working!" Yoffe writes of *The Longevity Project* (by Howard S. Friedman and Leslie R. Martin), a book on "Genetic Studies of Genius" that was begun in 1921 by Stanford University psychologist Lewis Terman.

Friedman and Martin write:

One of the most striking findings of The Longevity Project is that conscientiousness is a predictor of long life. People who blow their deadlines and forget their appointments tend to find themselves making an early appointment with the grim reaper. Sorting through eight decades of data shows that the reliable, more-mature-than-their-years little boys and girls identified in the 1920s became the dependable adults who were most likely to have made it into a new century.

The value of a life lived conscientiously might not show its effects early on, and so the dimension of *time* is clearly part of this understanding. What is needed is the ability to discern and uncover slowly *what is the reality* behind any situation that presents itself to our senses. There are certain principles that come to light as the invincible Miss Marple moves forward through each maze of disruptions and clues. For instance: Watch for both actions *and* their repetitions in the same person. "The pitcher mustn't go to the well too often." And do not forsake the rigors of the intellect: "One's feelings are not always reliable guidelines."

In many cases Miss Marple brings up comparative stories from the past of people she has known in St. Mary Mead. For instance, there is "Old Mrs. Pike's second boy, Alfred," now in a mental hospital after his mother had several close escapes from his dangerous actions. "Alfred *seemed* perfectly rational and normal. Almost painfully prosaic, if you know what I mean..." The realities beneath the surface, however, are often quite different.

Or there is the fact, she points out in *The Mirror Crack'd*, that a husband or wife is usually the most likely suspect in a murder case. But then again, the most *unlikely* person can also be the culprit. "I was speaking generally," said Miss Marple with dignity, nearly thinking aloud. She knows that there is not one easy solution or obvious tack that can always be followed to nab the killer. One must explore alternative routes within the mind, implementing logic, intelligence, and occasionally leaps of imagination almost akin to those required by Jesus' parables.

Such mental flexibility allows our elderly sleuth to see possibilities that may be hidden to the prosaic observer. Her method is often shown to be in contrast to the procedures of official inspectors, who are only too eager to jump to a conclusion and tie up a case. But in perhaps just as many cases, Miss Marple's special skills are appreciated by the experts, and she is invited to contribute openly in the quest for a solution.

Miss Marple respects intelligence and competence in others. But she is also wary of too-clever minds, as in the short story "Greenshaw's Folly": "... it reminded me of Mr. Naysmith," Miss Marple says in regard to a strange remark a suspect has made offhandedly. "He kept bees, and was very good at doing the acrostics in the Sunday papers. And he liked giving people false impressions just for fun. But sometimes it led to trouble."

In fact, the wayside, the stony ground, the thorns – and the Devil himself lurk just outside the perimeters, and they may even explain some of these stories of passion and temptation, subterfuge and distraction, false identities and misleading situations. The variety and cleverness of Agatha Christie's mysteries have made her the world's bestselling author, equaled only by the Bible and the works of Shakespeare.

Her unique creation, Miss Marple, of necessity must not only discern the mind of Christ in a situation for her own protection, dignity, and integrity. She also must in certain instances put herself mentally in the place of a perpetrator in order to feel out likely motives and envision possible deceptions. But it is only a temporary imaginative position. In the Old Testament Wisdom way of thinking, "Wisdom cannot take root in deceit, nor dwell in one given to exploiting others" (Wisdom of Solomon 1:4–5, tr. Rami Shapiro).

In *At Bertram's Hotel*, particularly, things are definitely not what they seem to be on the surface. In this story Miss Marple herself is almost swept up, accepting the artificial atmosphere that has been created to make certain clever crimes possible. She has to become alert to harsh realities that hide behind well-constructed easy chairs and perfect hotel service performed by impeccably costumed employees.

As a pampered recipient of this luxury for her duration at Bertram's, it would be easy for her eyes to be blinded to what these facades are hiding. But again, on this inner, knowing level the workings of logic and intuition prove to be of more import than the mind-lulling appearances and comforts she indulges in, even on a much-needed holiday.

Miss Marple is aware of what constitutes a fool, and looks for persons with these qualities to reveal themselves in circumstances that usually turn out to be cleverly constructed fronts:

> The wise are cautious and turn away from evil, but the fool throws off restraint and is careless.
>
> One who is quick-tempered acts foolishly, and the schemer is hated.
>
> The simple are adorned with folly, but the clever are crowned with knowledge.
>
> – Proverbs 14:16–18

It is the Parable of the Sower itself, through and through. And even in confusing circumstances, among skilled impersonators with troubled souls, Miss Marple once again finds herself up to the task of spiritual discernment and revelation.

Contemplating Christ in all things

For me, leading a contemplative life is being a person who sees the world as God sees the world; it is putting on the mind of God. The Scriptures are clear. "Put on ye the mind of Christ." What does this mean? Begin to think the way Jesus thought. Begin to think about life, about people, about issues, about everyday incidents the way Jesus thought about them. Jesus tells us over and over again how he thought about them. And he tells the leaders of the synagogue and of the state how he thought about them. Contemplation is an attitude of life... There is no substitute for it. Consciousness... of the presence of God – of the mind of God – of the will of God, and consciousness of God working in and through us.
– Joan Chittister in an interview (6/8/10)

Cowardice asks the question: is it safe? Expediency asks the question: is it politic? Vanity asks the question: is it popular? But conscience asks the question: is it right? And there comes a time when one must take a position that is neither safe, nor politic, nor popular – but one must take it simply because it is right.

– Martin Luther King, Jr.

Questions for Discussion:

1 What are some examples of situations you have encountered in which persons and situations have been revealed to be quite different from what you first assumed? How did you react in these cases? How did you discover the truth?

2 What specific qualities of Christ in the Gospels offer us the best guidelines for living the *conscious* and the *conscientious* life among others today?

3 Which stories and situations in the Miss Marple works most accurately embody these Christ-principles for you?

4 How can we grow in our ability to see beyond subtle untruths and the pitfalls of misleading circumstances without becoming cynical or distrusting of our neighbors – and thus forsaking love?

8

Love in Action Beyond St. Mary Mead

"Love, love – a frightening word."
– Miss Marple in *Nemesis*

To love another person is to see the face of God.
– Victor Hugo (lyric from *Les Miserables*)

Life is God's novel. Let Him write it.
– Isaac Bashevis Singer

A story is told about Mother Teresa's visit to the CEO of a large American corporation. She was begging money to expand her order into other parts of the world where the need was as great as in Calcutta.

This businessman received her graciously, but he said that his corporation could not give as generously as she had asked for. Mother Teresa then said, "Let us pray." Afterwards, the man still said no, but very politely.

Mother Teresa said again, "Let us pray." After about ten repetitions of this the CEO realized that she was NOT going to leave until he did what she asked. And he realized he couldn't throw her out – it would be terrible publicity and a public relations disaster.

And so, as she repeated, "Let us pray again," he said: "You know, Mother Teresa, I think you've got a point. I'll do it."

Even heavenly causes must be grounded in the real world. Karl Barth once said of Christians that they should keep the Bible in one hand and the daily newspaper in the other. And in the words of Rolf Gates, "We grow in our capacity to do the right thing each time we do the right thing."

In the last case of Miss Marple, *Nemesis* (although *Sleeping Murder* was published last, it had been written earlier, and chronologically *Sleeping Murder* fits between *The Moving Finger* and *The Mirror Crack'd*) we find perhaps the most fleshed-out philosophy behind the Christ-imitation she has practiced in discipline and love, throughout a long and deeply engaged life with others.

Nemesis unfolds, as does real life, in confusing and piecemeal fashion, so that Miss Marple herself does not know exactly what she is doing, why she is with the particular people who make up the scenario of this case, or what it is she is supposed to uncover. *Nemesis* offers the reader an opportunity to share from her point of view the frustrations of a human life lived *without* the omniscient viewpoint that sometimes ties together the narrative structure of a novel.

Even though her health is frail and she seems to need more rest than she used to – and her nephew's wife has told her, "Don't get mixed up in any more murders" – she is drawn to the center of a new intrigue by a letter "from the grave".

While reading the obituary column in her newspaper, she learns that the wealthy gentleman, Jason Rafiel, whom she had met and collaborated with in *A Caribbean Mystery*, has died. As it was a while ago, the name strikes a bell, but at first she can't place him.

But her memory of their association, more than a year previous, returns, and she reflects on what might have happened to some of the other principals in the case that she and Mr. Rafiel jointly solved. But soon she puts it out of her mind and thinks of their association in terms of "ships that pass in the night", of temporary allies who moved on.

But the story underlines the fact that all of our acts, especially when done in the proper spirit, have consequences far beyond what we can imagine or predict. Her ministrations of concern for those closest to her, through the various cases, had already expanded to include that 'working vacation' on a Caribbean island, helping to ferret out the truth.

Now that past association with Mr. Rafiel will take her into circles beyond St. Mary Mead for purposes that the old man designed before his death. He had discerned the depth of her character and her skill, and determined that she was the person to set even the past in proper perspective – in ways she will discover after responding to a letter from the dead man's solicitors.

When she is asked by one of the solicitors handling the case that is *Nemesis*, "Have you had... any connection with crime or the investigation of crime?" she answers: "Strictly speaking I should say no. Nothing professional, that is to say. I have never been a probation officer or indeed sat as a magistrate on a bench or been connected in any way with a detective agency." Completely true – but far from the whole story. And just as she was a "nemesis" or undefeatable opponent of evil in *A Caribbean Mystery*, so in this last story will she prove up to the task again. (Though the evoking of associations with Nemesis as "she who distributes or deals out", the Greek goddess of indignation and retribution, seems intentionally extreme.)

And just as, in Miss Marple's world, "truth will out"; just so, *love* will not be constrained in the world when it is embodied by a willing Christ-bearer. And so when the right offer is made to bring about her involvement in a years-old mistaken arrest (or was it?) – Miss Marple, even through her doubts, is on board. She cannot deny her identification with those who have suffered through the cruelty of others, or her personal concern for a possible miscarriage of justice, no matter how far in the distant past.

"You have a natural flair for justice, and that has led to your having a natural flair for crime," she reads in Mr. Rafiel's posthumous letter in *Nemesis*. As he had said when evaluating Miss Marple earlier in *A Caribbean Mystery*: "I've been wrong about her... All knitting wool and tittle-tattle. But this one's got something. Eyes and ears, and she uses them."

Miss Marple can hardly prevent herself from becoming entangled in mysteries involving crimes or potential threats, just as she finds it difficult to refrain from exerting her pruning skills in other people's neglected gardens. "Miss Marple's hands could hardly restrain themselves from pulling up the vagrant bindweed asserting its superiority" when visiting the garden of three mysterious sisters while staying as their house guest during the unfolding of *Nemesis*.

So when Mr. Rafiel's solicitors ask that she consider the proposition he left her in a letter before he died, she is at first reticent, protesting, "I am a very simple person." And it is easy to see in the lines of the story that this 'simplicity' – a love of duty, the habit of sensible actions, and the intelligence to carry her successfully through whatever life will next demand of her – exactly qualifies her for the job.

When she accepts the letter from the solicitors, addressed to "Miss Jane Marple, resident in the village of St. Mary Mead", it is clear that Mr. Rafiel has made note of her availability to be contacted exactly where she regularly does the most good: in her own home and village.

In Mr. Rafiel's words:

I envisage you sitting in a chair [and she is]... that is agreeable and comfortable for whatever kind or form of rheumatism from which you may suffer... I see you, as I saw you once one night as I rose from sleep disturbed by your urgency, in a cloud of pink wool... If you prefer to continue knitting, that is your decision. If you prefer to serve the cause of justice, I hope that you may at least find it interesting.

And at the end of the letter he quotes appropriately from the book of the Old Testament Prophet Amos: "Let justice roll down like waters and righteousness like an everlasting stream." Clearly this finale is to be a redemptive story with far-reaching implications.

Charles Dickens once wrote that: "Charity begins at home and justice begins next door." Miss Marple is deeply aware of the first truth; and her modest travels and trips venturing outside the comfort of St. Mary Mead have also convinced her of the second part of this maxim – since the world itself begins "next door" in terms of her calling.

As she mulls over Mr. Rafiel's proposal that she take on an unspelled-out puzzle, trusting that she will be given guidance on the path as she needs it, "It was only then that it occurred to her suddenly that without noticing it she had definitely accepted the mandate."

Her acceptance occurs in a multi-layered 'atmosphere' which she addresses directly – in the absence of the man who had made the request in the letter: "I believe in eternal life," said Miss Marple. "I don't know exactly where you are, Mr. Rafiel, but I have no doubt that you are *somewhere* – I will do my best to fulfill your wishes."

Miss Marple's spirituality is all about love in action. In 1 Corinthians 13, the 'love chapter' the Apostle Paul lists the qualities that describe this greatest attribute a Christian can embody:

> Love is patient; love is kind; love is not envious or boastful or arrogant or rude... It does not rejoice in wrongdoing, but rejoices in the truth.
> (vv. 4–6)

As F.B. Meyer once wrote of this famous passage:

> Jesus sits for His portrait in these glowing sentences, and every clause is true of Him. Substitute His name for 'love'

throughout the chapter, and see whether it is not an exact likeness.

Love, truth, and justice are indelibly linked. As Elie Wiesel, a Holocaust survivor, put it:

> I swore never to be silent whenever and wherever human beings endure suffering and humiliation. We must always take sides. Neutrality helps the oppressor, never the victim. Silence encourages the tormenter, never the tormented. Sometimes we must interfere when human lives are in danger, when human dignity is in danger.

This also could describe the vision for love-in-action that will take Miss Marple outside of her personal environs and into the threatening world that surrounds St. Mary Mead (though, as we've seen in previous cases, even a small village does not lack examples of all the deadly sins in force).

In *Nemesis*, the vigilant Mr. Rafiel has arranged that Miss Marple (whom he felt certain *would* take the case) will have the protection and support of some "guardian angels" – though they are so well disguised that the reader and Miss Marple herself will remain unsure whom to trust until very late in the story.

Love may be pure and single-minded in its intentions and operations in the world, especially seen as an *aspect* of Christ, or as *Christ himself*. But the ways in which it permeates and transforms situations is far from simple or easily predicted. Thus the Christian is encouraged to abandon himself or herself to Love rather than ever to seek to control it, even for the best-intended purposes. The Apostle Paul even urges Christians in Galatians 5:13 to "through love become slaves to one another." Yet truly it is love that sets us free.

Miss Marple, with her feminine sensibilities that are so much a part of her character, her incarnation and presence in the world, poignantly embodies this paradox. As Khalil Gibran (*The Prophet*) simply stated it: "Think not you can direct the course of love, for love, if it finds you worthy, directs your course."

Dallas Willard has written in *The Renovaré Spiritual Formation Bible*:

> Jesus founded on earth a new type of community, and in it and through him love – God-given agape love – came down to live with power on earth. Now, it is this God-given agape love that transforms our lives and gives us true spiritual substance as persons... We could call this the 1 Corinthians 13 Test: "If I... understand all mysteries and all knowledge, and if I have all faith, so as to remove mountains, but do not have love, I am nothing" (v. 2). And so the test of whether we have really gotten the point of the Bible would then be the quality of love we show.

Miss Marple, seeking to embody love/justice in her own God-given life, finds that its course, like that of romantic love, "seldom runs smooth". But her overarching dedication to duty, and her acceptance of what a dedicated life may require of her, keep her on its paths.

The Miss Marple novels themselves could almost be 'graphed' or charted according to the presence of spiritual love or its lack in the various characters and situations.

The dramatic arc of a story can be described in terms of exposition, rising action, climax, falling action, and dénouement. Julian Symons in his book *Mortal Consequences: A History from the Detective Story to the Crime Novel*, quotes Joseph Wood Krutch, who in 1944 called the detective story "the one clearly defined modern genre of prose fiction impeccably classical in form."

The Miss Marple mysteries exhibit various patterns usually consisting of these elements: a murder, act of violence, or threat; suspicious behavior in a multitude of characters; unsuspected twists and behind-the-scenes manipulations; and, woven through the plot, Miss Marple's contribution to the solving of a complicated life puzzle.

Greek philosopher Aristotle wrote in *The Poetics* that: "The whole is what has a beginning and middle and end." These three clearly identified sections, as we live through them with the characters, make the mysteries a complete and satisfying experience. And throughout, Miss Marple's example of love which reveals her character (and that of others) consistently illuminates the events, adds to meanings, and helps us make connections in the story that we were unable to see before. Sometimes her ingenious solutions could almost be said to be 'spiritually discerned'.

Jesus calls real men and real women, with complex emotions and intellects, to live and work in the midst of sometimes gritty situations. Although we ourselves may encounter these challenges in a variety of modes and at various levels, some of our own stories, as God 'writes them', can be compared, contrasted, and looked back to for meaning. Such reflection may confirm for us the absolute sureness of God's call for us to 'take heed' – to plunge in and put our own love into action wherever we are called to go.

Who is in your personal cast of characters? What is your attitude toward these others?

Dietrich Bonhoeffer has written in his *Letters and Papers from Prison* (1945):

The person who despises another will never be able to make anything of him. Nothing that we despise in the other is entirely absent from ourselves. ... We must learn to regard people less in the light of what they do or omit to do, and more in the light of what they suffer. The only profitable relationship to others – and especially to our weaker brethren – is one of love, and that means the will to hold fellowship with them. God did not despise humanity, but became human for our sake.

How will we choose to take love into the world beyond our own comfort zone, until "Christ is all in all"?

Love is eternal

Everything that has existed, lingers in the Eternity.
– Agatha Christie

The man who has found love eats and drinks Christ every day and hour, and hereby is made immortal. "He that eateth of this bread," [Christ] says, "which I will give to him, shall not see death unto eternity." Blessed is he who consumes the bread of love, which is Jesus!... Wherefore, the man who lives in love reaps the fruit of life from God, and while yet in this world, he even now breathes the air of the resurrection.
– Saint Isaak of Syria

If we take the Gospels seriously, we are left, in our dire predicament, facing an utterly humbling question: How must we live and work so as not to be estranged from God's presence in his work and in all his creatures? The answer, we may say, is given in Jesus' teaching about love. But that answer raises another question that plunges us into the abyss of our ignorance, which is both human and peculiarly modern: How are we to make of that love an economic practice? That question calls for many answers, and we don't know most of them. It is a question that those humans who want to answer it will be living and working with for a long time – if they are allowed a long time. Meanwhile, may heaven guard us from those who think they already have the answers.
– Wendell Berry in "The Burden of the Gospels" (9/20/05)

Questions for Discussion:

1 How are love and justice in the world intimately entwined? What are the implications of this for the Christian who is contemplating a specific action toward another person?

2 In what practical ways are we called to 'take Jesus' into our lives, within our Christian community, and to the world?

3 What does a human being "clothed" in love look like?

4 In what ways is the spiritual quality of love or charity eternal?

A Woman for Our Times

Life is meant to be lived from a Center, a divine Center. Each one of us can live such a life of amazing power and peace and serenity, of integration and confidence and simplified multiplicity, on one condition – that is, if we really want to.
– Thomas R. Kelly in *A Testament of Devotion*

For age is opportunity no less
Than youth itself, though in another dress,
And as the evening twilight fades away
The sky is filled with stars, invisible by day.
– Henry Wadsworth Longfellow

Professional detectives are no match for elderly spinsters.
– Agatha Christie at the publication of *The Body in the Library*

If you open for me a space the size of a needle, I will open for you the width of the sea.
– Talmud saying

It may at first seem odd even to suggest that the elderly, fluttering Miss Marple with her knitting, gardening, and "interfering" could be a model for spiritual living in our time. Yet, in her own words: "Human nature… is very much the same everywhere. It is more difficult to observe it closely in a city, that is all."

Perhaps the exact parameters of human nature are less agreed on today, in a postmodern world. But I contend that much that is timeless in her character and her loving, intelligent actions can still shine out for us as we seek, with her, to model our own lives on Christ.

In this book, I have striven to take her as she is presented to us in the twelve novels and twenty short stories, observing (as she herself would) the facts, what others say about her, and the overwhelming effects of her actions revealed through a series of difficult and mysterious time-sensitive situations.

The books are, after all, products of their time, ranging in publication dates from 1930–1976, and often harking back to even earlier twentieth-century situations than are reflected in their year of publication. And within their pages we admittedly will find cultural prejudices, and even a few pejorative appellations we no longer approve of in public discourse – some of which, admittedly, meant something quite different to Christie's contemporary audience.

For instance (avoiding the worst of these in print, even here), Christie plays into the contemporary disdain apparently shared by her audience for young women who are "bottle-blondes" — and especially those with "adenoidal" accents (perhaps they just had nasal problems?). One can only imagine what Miss Marple would think of the extremes of beauty aids and cosmetic surgery today. In *A Murder Is Announced,* she refers to a Wesleyan minister who wouldn't let his daughter wear a "plate on her teeth. Said it was the Lord's Will if her teeth stuck out."

But these petty quibbles aside, there is much in the Miss Marple mysteries that is universal and lasting in the portrayal of human nature, of the likely manifestations of good and evil, and of a way to live productively into old age. Jane Marple herself illustrates in exquisite particularity how the Christ-life can be lived through discipline, by attention to facts, and especially in loving concern for the needs and problems of others, in whatever circumstances one finds oneself, provincial or cosmopolitan.

This elderly spinster, who could be any of our aunts or solitary neighbors, accepts herself for who she is. She once remarks that, although another friend her age lives her life at *presto* – if each person's life has a "tempo" – Miss Marple is "content to be adagio." No one disputes the oft-repeated fact: "She's old, but she's sharp."

Can we even envision a spiritually robust and fruitfully rich old age, with our own era's clear bias toward the desirability of youth and blatantly overt sexuality coming at us in words and pictures, seemingly from every corner?

Jesus declared in John 10:10: "I came that they may have life, and have it abundantly." But how many people do we know who embody this fulfillment of soul? I nominate Miss Marple for Christlike role model as a woman for our times.

No one who spends the tens of hours required to read all of the Christie works on Miss Marple, I contend, will come away seeing either her spinsterhood, her age, her quirks, or her "reduced circumstances" as constituting a hindrance to this view. And none of these traits, including her plain, ordinary face and simple cottage, would ever be anything she would either apologize for, or allow to be a deterrent in her social obligations or in living a meaningful, fulfilled life.

She lives abundantly, wisely, amid post-war scarcity, often among difficult people, in the midst of dangerous situations, while being treated condescendingly by certain neighbors, housekeepers, and policemen – yet her dignity and sense of purpose never falter.

From where does her wholeness come? She dwells clearly from the "divine" center of "amazing power and peace and serenity," as quoted by Thomas R. Kelly above (in *A Testament of Devotion*, 1941). And her character as revealed in the novels shows us how to do so as well.

Our wills are ours, we know not how;
Our wills are ours, to make them thine.

wrote Alfred, Lord Tennyson in the Prologue of *In Memoriam*

(1904).

> Our little systems have their day;
> They have their day and cease to be:
> They are but broken lights of thee,
> And thou, O Lord, art more than they.
> We have but faith: we cannot know;
> For knowledge is of things we see;
> And yet we trust it comes from thee,
> A beam in darkness: let it grow.

Of the many descriptions that are possible to metaphorically convey the nature and impact of this 'woman for all seasons' – a "beam in darkness" is surely a simple but excellent one. It is reminiscent of Jesus' injunction in Matthew 5:16 to "let your light shine before others, so that they may see your good works and give glory to your Father in heaven."

One of my favorite lines from Shakespeare is found in *The Merchant of Venice*: "How far that little candle throws his beams! So shines a good deed in a naughty world ..."

Jesus himself is called the Light of the world in John 8:12 – and so are his followers in Matthew 5:14: "You are the light of the world" – intended to give "light to all in the house" (v. 15). This accomplishment Miss Marple attains nearly literally, as her quiet pronouncements and confident conclusions shine light on the most hidden and confusing aspects of each case.

It is said of one character in *They Do It with Mirrors* that "He wanted to be God. He forgot that man is only the humble instrument of God's will." Seeking to live the God-life is a precarious undertaking, and poses inevitable dangers of falling into pride and arrogance. "People who can be very good can be very bad too," Miss Marple once observes.

She often mirrors the "mother hen" that Jesus is compared to in Luke 13:34, in her desire to gather innocent people "under her wings" for their own safety. Yet even this is not without contro-versy. Should she expect of others this level of sacrifice that she is willing to offer?

When, in *The Moving Finger*, Miss Marple engages the help of a young woman in solving the case, the narrator of that book tells her:

"There's one thing I can't forgive you for, Miss Marple – roping in [the young woman]."

We read that Miss Marple put down her crocheting and looked at him over her spectacles with stern (and confident) eyes. "My dear young man, *something* had to be done… I found the person I needed [to prove her case]."

"It was dangerous for her."

"Yes, it was dangerous, but we are not put into this world, Mr. Burton, to avoid danger when an innocent fellow-creature's life is at stake."

Miss Marple is at one with herself on her own reasons for risking life, for remaining of sound mind, ready and willing to use her diminishing physical strength for as long as she is able to do so. *Someone had to do something.*

Criminals frequently found her to be just the stumbling-stone that would trip them up in their path of crime. It is no wonder that even in these controversies and disagreements about her methods, not uncommon in the mysteries, she also mirrors Jesus, who was the cornerstone of the faith to believers, but was to others a stumbling-block that they could neither accept nor get around.

In Luke 18 a "certain ruler" comes to Jesus to ask what he must do to obtain eternal life. Though the man has striven to keep the law blamelessly, Jesus requires one more thing of him: "Sell all that you own and distribute the money to the poor, and you will have treasure in heaven" (v. 22). Though there is no indication that this is an injunction for *everyone* to follow, the requirement clearly constituted a stumbling-block for this young man, who was very rich. "Indeed, it is easier for a camel to go through the eye of a needle," we read, than for such a rich person to submit to giving away everything.

Jesus and his unrelenting standards are compared to a "living stone" in 1 Peter 2:4. He is the one who in his earthly life was "rejected by mortals yet chosen and precious in God's sight" (v. 4). It is clear that he is the standard and the center itself for all in this early Christian community who have faith. But to those who cannot accept his radical requirements, he is "a stone that makes them stumble, and a rock that makes them fall" (v. 8). He is either a sanctuary, or a trap (cf. Isaiah 8:14–15). The same stone, but a different reaction to him brings a different result, much as the sun melts butter but hardens clay.

And in her conscientiousness and consistency when it comes to combating evil, Miss Marple herself is both a trap to some, and a touchstone to others. "Miss Marple is usually right. That's what makes her unpopular," comments the Rev. Leonard Clement in *The Murder at the Vicarage*. Just so. And just as Christ himself stood with the outcast and the suffering.

Lewis B. Smedes wrote in *How Can It Be All Right When Everything Is All Wrong*:

> Jesus still puts himself into the shoes of anyone who suffers. If you want to know who the vicar of Christ is, find yourself a hurting human being in your neighborhood. Jesus is found where people are putting up with things they want to go away, trying to cope when everything is all wrong. He is represented on earth by the wounded. He is not among them as a visitor, not even as a comforting friend. He is one of them; he is any or all of them… Jesus points to suffering people and says, "There I am. "… Jesus is your hurting neighbor. He is your hurting child. He is your hurting enemy. He is anyone who is suffering from anything not of his or her own choosing. If you feel the hurt of any person who hurts, you are

suffering with Jesus.

Throughout the Miss Marple stories, a number of biblical terms are used in comparison and contrast, to add another layer of meaning to the twentieth-century characters and their actions: walls of Jericho; holy of holies; Garden of Eden/serpent. Consider the prodigal son/older brother theme in *A Pocket Full of Rye*: "Percy and I never got on... I blew my pocket money, he saved his." These overlaps with biblical parable and story, setting and message, further strengthen the spiritual meanings that lie below the surface (and could be treated in another study of biblical meaning in Agatha Christie novels).

But our focus here is: How does Miss Marple fulfill the ideal of being a "little Christ" in the "whirlpool of life" (as it is referred to) among her fellow humans? Perhaps in one surprising way. She has found the secret of *joy*, even with her physical limitations (though "her long distance sight was good, as many of her neighbors knew to their cost in the village of St. Mary Mead"): advancing age, and other frailties – and no doubt loneliness, disappointments, and even betrayals over the decades.

At the end of *Nemesis*, a solicitor who has been assisting with the case suddenly thinks he sees, for a fleeting moment, superimposed on the elderly visage of Miss Marple: "a vague impression of a young and pretty girl shaking hands with the vicar at a garden party in the country."

What could this golden moment recollected in memory from a truly peak experience in his youth – of a young girl happily going off to enjoy her life – possibly have in common with a gently triumphant elderly sleuth at the end of a case that has brought her unprecedented monetary reward?

There is no other way to identify what she embodies than as the "peace that passes understanding" (Phil 4:7) and the "joy of the redeemed" (Isaiah 35) – brimming from her plain, honest expression. Critic A.N. Wilson called Miss Marple "a more impressive creation than those old women such as Mrs. Moore in the novels of E.M. Forster, who are somehow meant to carry quasi-mythic weight and hidden wisdom."

The Greek philosopher Solon famously pronounced: "Call no man happy until his life is over." Author Paul Woodruff comments on this maxim in *Reverence: Renewing a Forgotten Virtue*: "By this he meant that a human life is too uncertain to be judged on the basis of any part of it: no one can safely claim to be living a totally successful life." But in these last snapshots that we have of our heroine, as Miss Marple is thinking of being able to buy the small pleasures she had denied herself for so long, we identify a life that is happy and fulfilled, perhaps as clearly as we ever will.

> The days of our life are seventy years, or perhaps eighty, if we are strong; even then their span is only toil and trouble...
> Teach us to count our days that we may gain a wise heart.
> – Psalm 90:10, 12.

Time is a commodity in which we are immersed as humans, and we are meant to use it to its end, until the last grains of sand fall to the bottom of the hourglass. "The essence of life is going forward. Life is really a One Way Street, isn't it?" Miss Marple comments in *At Bertram's Hotel*.

At the end of *Nemesis*, instead of choosing to put her reward money into a savings account for a "rainy day", Miss Marple asserts: "The only thing I shall want for a rainy day will be my umbrella." Instead, she has other pleasures in mind. "I'm going to spend it, you know. I'm going to have some fun with it."

What specifically does she have in mind?

"Partridges," Miss Marple said thoughtfully. "It is very difficult to get partridges nowadays, and they're very expensive. I should enjoy a partridge – a whole partridge – to myself, very much."

Thus does Miss Marple's anticipated partridge dinner

foreshadow the final banquet of the redeemed, the Supper of the Lamb – where we envision a most-honored place set for her at the table.

The meaning of a Christian life

Thou thyself must go through Christ's whole journey, and enter wholly into his process.
– Jacob Boehme

All of you, every *one* of you – will pass through a time when you will face despair. If you never face despair, you will never have faced, or become, a Christian, or known a Christian life. To be a Christian you must face and accept the life that Christ faced and lived; you must enjoy things as he enjoyed things; be as happy as he was at the marriage at Cana, know the peace and happiness that it means to be at harmony with God and with God's will. But you must also know, as he did, what it means to be alone in the Garden of Gethsemane, to feel that all your friends have forsaken you, that those you love and trust have turned away from you, and that *God Himself* has forsaken you. Hold on then to the belief that that is *not* the end. If you love, you will suffer, and if you do not love, you do not know the meaning of a Christian life.
– Agatha Christie in *An Autobiography* (her recollection of a favorite teacher's words)

The world is not comprehensible, but it is embraceable: through the embracing of one of its beings.
– Martin Buber

The human spirit is the lamp of the Lord.
– Proverbs 20:27

Notes

Introduction

New Revised Standard Version Bible, copyright 1989, Division of Christian Education of the National Council of the Churches of Christ in the United States of America. Used by permission. All rights reserved.

The Life and Times of Miss Jane Marple (New York: Berkley Books, 1987) p. 84

"The Thumbmark of St. Peter" in *The Tuesday Club Murders* (NY: Dell, 1975) p. 75

The New York Times, "Girls and Boys Together" by Gail Collins (March 2, 2011)

Chapter 1

The Body in the Library (*Miss Marple Omnibus*, New York: Harper Collins, 1997) parish committees, pp. 134–135

The Life and Times of Miss Jane Marple (New York: Berkley Books, 1987) p. 84

Thomas à Kempis (ca. 1380–1471) *The Imitation of Christ*

The Divine Feminine in Biblical Wisdom Literature (Woodstock, VT: Skylight Paths, 2005) p. 133

Chapter 2

Becoming Fully Human (New York: Sheed and Ward, 2005) p. 115

The Lady Investigates: Women Detectives and Spies in Fiction (New York: St. Martin's Press, 1981) p. 179

Solitude (New York: The Free Press, 1988) p. 94

Traits of a Healthy Spirituality (Mystic, CT: Twenty-Third Publications, 2005) p. 35

Bede Griffiths edited by Peter Spink (Springfield, IL: Templegate Publishers, 2003) p. 57

Heart: A Personal Journey Through Its Myths and Meanings (New

York: William Morrow) p. 81

Chapter 3

Tales of the Hasidim (New York: Schocken Books, 1948)

The Monist, Vol. 86, Issue 3, 2003

How to Believe Again (Minneapolis: Fortress Press, 1972)

John Stott in "The Quotable Stott", *Christianity Today* (April 2, 2001)

The Dalai Lama, quoted in the *Huffington Post* by Anita Thompson (7/27/08)

Chapter 4

Gospel Medicine (Boston: Cowley Publications, 1995) p. 153

Six Walks in the Fictional Woods (Cambridge, MA: Harvard University Press, 1998) p. 91

Flowers in the Desert: A Spirituality of the Bible (New York: Paulist Press, 1987) pp. 39–40

Chapter 5

Once to Every Man and Nation by James Russell Lowell (1819–1891) was published in the *Boston Courier* on December 11, 1845. It was written as a protest to America's war with Mexico and was later put to music by Thomas J. William in 1890 to the tune of *Ebenezer*.

The Divine Feminine in Biblical Wisdom Literature (Woodstock, VT: Skylight Paths, 2005) p. 130

Shroud for the Archbishop (New York: Signet, 1998)

Uncommon Gratitude: Alleluia for All That Is (Collegeville, MN: Liturgical Press, 2010) p. 125

Chapter 6

Parables: The Arrows of God (Maryknoll, NY: Orbis Books, 1994) pp. 24, 25

Chapter 7

Negotiating with the Dead (New York: Anchor, 2003) p. 174

Creation Continues (Mahwah: NJ: Paulist Press, 1987)

The Devil's Dictionary (New York: Bloomsbury USA, 2004) p. 89

Article in *Slate* by Emily Yoffe (3/10/11) "Don't Stop Working!"

Chapter 8

The Prophet (New York: Alfred A. Knopf, 1964) p. 14

The Renovaré Spiritual Formation Bible (HarperSanFrancisco, 2005)
   p. xxvi

*Mortal Consequences. A History from the Detective Story to the Crime
   Novel* (New York: Schocken Books, 1972) p. 2

Letters and Papers from Prison (New York: Touchstone, 1997) p. 10

"The Burden of the Gospels" in the *Christian Century* (9/20/05)

Chapter 9

A Testament of Devotion (New York: HarperOne, 1996) p. 93

How Can It Be All Right When Everything Is All Wrong? (Wheaton,
   IL: Shaw Books, 2000) p. 93

Reverence: Renewing a Forgotten Virtue (Oxford University Press,
   2001) p. 82

Partridges: Stefanie Goyette has written in *Feminism and Religion*
   (6/9/12) that "In medieval culture, partridges are coded as a
   hot food, as an aristocratic food, and as 'man food'." Is
   Christie hinting here at a nearly forbidden pleasure?

Agatha Christie: An Autobiography (New York: Dodd, Mead &
   Company, 1977) p. 139

Bibliography

à Kempis, Thomas. *The Imitation of Christ.* ca. 1380–1471

Bonhoeffer, Dietrich. *Letters and Papers from Prison.* New York: Touchstone, 1997

Buber, Martin. *Tales of the Hasidim.* New York: Schocken Books, 1948

Chittister, Joan. *Becoming Fully Human.* New York: Sheed and Ward, 2005

Chittister, Joan and Williams, Rowan. *Uncommon Gratitude: Alleluia for All That Is.* Collegeville, MN: Liturgical Press, 2010

Christie, Agatha. *Agatha Christie: An Autobiography.* New York: Dodd, Mead & Company, 1977

Christie, Agatha. *Miss Marple Meets Murder: The Mirror Crack'd. A Pocket Full of Rye. At Bertram's Hotel. The Moving Finger.* Garden City, NY: Nelson Doubleday, Inc, 1980

Christie, Agatha. *Miss Marple Omnibus: The Body in the Library. The Moving Finger. A Murder Is Announced. 4.50 from Paddington.* New York: Harper Collins, 1997

Christie, Agatha. *Miss Marple: The Complete Short Stories.* New York: G.P. Putnam's Sons, 1985

Christie, Agatha. *Postmark Murder: A Caribbean Mystery. Nemesis.* Garden City, NY: Nelson Doubleday, Inc 1986

Christie, Agatha. *Sleeping Murder.* New York: Signet, 2000

Christie, Agatha. *The Murder at the Vicarage.* New York: Berkley Books, 1984

Christie, Agatha. *The Tuesday Club Murders.* New York: Dell, 1975

Christie, Agatha. *They Do It with Mirrors.* New York: Signet, 2000

Craig, Patricia. Cadogan, Mary. *The Lady Investigates: Women Detectives and Spies in Fiction.* New York: St. Martin's Press, 1981

Dumm, Demetrius. *Flowers in the Desert: A Spirituality of the Bible.* New York: Paulist Press, 1987

Eco, Umberto. *Six Walks in the Fictional Woods*. Cambridge, MA: Harvard University Press, 1998

Foster, Richard. Willard, Dallas. Brueggemann, Walter. Peterson, Eugene H. *The Renováré Spiritual Formation Bible*. HarperSanFrancisco, 2005

Griffiths, Bede. *Bede Griffiths*, edited by Peter Spink. Springfield, IL: Templegate Publishers, 2003

Hart, Anne. *The Life and Times of Miss Jane Marple*. New York: Berkley Books, 1987

Kelly, Thomas R. *A Testament of Devotion*. New York: HarperOne, 1996

Kunkel, Fritz. *Creation Continues*. Mahwah: N J: Paulist Press, 1987

McKenna, Megan. *Parables: The Arrows of God*. Maryknoll, NY: Orbis Books, 1994

Shapiro, Rabbi Rami. *The Divine Feminine in Biblical Wisdom Literature*. Woodstock, VT: Skylight Paths, 2005

Shaw, Marion. Vanacker, Sabine. *Reflecting on Miss Marple*. London and New York: Routledge, 1991

Smedes, Lewis B. *How Can It Be All Right When Everything Is All Wrong?* Wheaton, IL: Shaw Books, 2000

Storr, Anthony. *Solitude*. New York: The Free Press, 1988

Svoboda, Melannie. *Traits of a Healthy Spirituality*. Mystic, CT: Twenty-Third Publications, 2005

Symons, Julian. *Mortal Consequences*. New York: Schocken Books, 1972

Taylor, Barbara Brown. *Gospel Medicine*. Boston: Cowley Publications, 1995

Thielicke, Helmut. *How to Believe Again*. Minneapolis: Fortress Press, 1972

Tremayne, Peter. *Shroud for the Archbishop*. New York: Signet, 1998

Waldron, Jeremy. *The Monist*. Vol. 86, Issue 3. 2003

Woodruff, Paul. *Reverence: Renewing a Forgotten Virtue*. Oxford University Press, 2001

Never Underestimate Miss Marple

It's just too difficult to imagine detective fiction without Jane Marple (black lace mittens, knitting needles and all) in its pantheon of greats.
– *USA Today*

Miss Marple is a kind of social conscience: "The detective story was... very much a story with a moral... the hunting down of Evil, and the triumph of Good."
– Marion Shaw & Sabine Vanacker quoting Agatha Christie in *Reflecting on Miss Marple*

... a more impressive creation than those old women such as Mrs. Moore in the novels of E.M. Forster, who are somehow meant to carry quasi-mythic weight and hidden wisdom.
– A.N. Wilson

The Marple novels are the folktales of twentieth-century suburban life, and Miss Marple herself is the presiding genius, the good fairy, and guide...
– From *Reflecting on Miss Marple*

"Just the finest detective God ever made – natural genius cultivated in a suitable soul... [an] elderly lady... at the top of the class."
– Sir Henry Clithering in *4.50 from Paddington*

I think it's significant that very early dramas were known as mysteries. They dealt in a more human way than the Scriptures or church services with sacred subjects and matters of good and evil.
– Ross Macdonald

If some Christians question whether a mystery story can be a Christian story, they do not know their own faith thoroughly enough.

– William David Spencer in *Mysterium and Mystery: The Clerical Crime Novel*

Also by this Author

Spinning Straw, Weaving Gold: A Tapestry of Mother-Daughter
Wisdom

Becoming Flame: Uncommon Mother-Daughter Wisdom
–Foreword by Phyllis Tickle

Awaiting the Child: An Advent Journal
–Introduction by Madeleine L'Engle

Soul Moments: Times When Heaven Touches Earth

40-Day Journey with Madeleine L'Engle

Blessings and Prayers for Married Couples

Simple Blessings for Sacred Moments

Co-Authored with Diane Marquart Moore:
Chant of Death

Circle Books

Circle is a symbol of infinity and unity. It's part of a growing list of imprints, including o-books.net and zero-books.net.

Circle Books aims to publish books in Christian spirituality that are fresh, accessible, and stimulating.

Our books are available in all good English language bookstores worldwide. If you can't find the book on the shelves, then ask your bookstore to order it for you, quoting the ISBN and title. Or, you can order online—all major online retail sites carry our titles.

To see our list of titles, please view www.Circle-Books.com, growing by 80 titles per year.

Authors can learn more about our proposal process by going to our website and clicking on Your Company > Submissions.

We define Christian spirituality as the relationship between the self and its sense of the transcendent or sacred, which issues in literary and artistic expression, community, social activism, and practices. A wide range of disciplines within the field of religious studies can be called upon, including history, narrative studies, philosophy, theology, sociology, and psychology. Interfaith in approach, Circle Books fosters creative dialogue with non-Christian traditions.

And tune into MySpiritRadio.com for our book review radio show, hosted by June-Elleni Laine, where you can listen to authors discussing their books.

MySpiritRadio